APPEASEMENT BEFORE, DURING AND AFTER THE WAR

APPEASEMENT
BEFORE, DURING AND
AFTER THE WAR

BY

PAUL EINZIG

MACMILLAN AND CO., LIMITED
ST. MARTIN'S STREET, LONDON
1942

" It is always a temptation for a rich and lazy nation
To puff and look important and to say :—
' Though we know we should defeat you,
We have not the time to meet you.
We will therefore pay you cash to go away.'

And that is called paying the Danegeld :
But we've proved it again and again,
That if once you have paid him the Danegeld
You never get rid of the Dane."

RUDYARD KIPLING, *Paying the Danegeld*

PREFACE

I AM in favour of well-established lasting peace after this war. Therefore I am against appeasement. It is my contention that the tragic error of judgment of those who in the past believed in the possibility of inducing Hitler by means of appeasement to abandon his aggressive designs has a large share in the responsibility for the present war. And it is my contention that those who imagine that after this war peace in the true sense of the term can be bought at the price of appeasement unwittingly prepare the ground for another disastrous war. They fail to grasp the teachings of recent history which conclusively show the failure of the policy of appeasement.

Although appeasement has been one of the most discussed topics during the last few years, strangely enough no one has yet undertaken to produce a book covering the whole wide range of the subject. It is true appeasement has a vast literature. Most of the thousands of books written about it are confined, however, to describing and criticising the major acts of political appeasement in recent years. The economic aspects of appeasement have been largely ignored. This is because appeasement in the economic sphere is not nearly as spectacular as in the political sphere. No act of appeasement can compare in dramatic effect with the Munich surrender, for instance. Although in some cases, such as the Czech gold scandal, the Düsseldorf deal, and the £1000 million loan scheme, economic appeasement received its due share of publicity, the broader significance of these individual acts of economic appeasement was largely overlooked.

In order to make good the one-sidedness of literature on appeasement this book is devoted mainly, though by no means exclusively, to describing and criticising the policy of economic appeasement. I shall try to make readers realise the consistency of purpose that ran through apparently isolated individual acts of economic appeasement. While any one act of economic appeasement may appear insignificant in comparison with any of the major acts of political appeasement, it will be seen that the combined weight of acts of economic appeasement was very considerable. The desire to redress the balance between the amount of attention paid to economic and political appeasement is, however, not the only justification I claim for writing this book. The main reason for my decision to publish it is the necessity to dispel the widespread illusion that appeasement is dead and buried. Most writers on the subject are inclined to talk about appeasement in the past tense. They and their readers assume that appeasement came to an end with the outbreak of the war. If this were so it would be difficult to justify the publication of this book at the present moment, when in the interest of the war effort recriminations for the past should be avoided whenever possible. It is for this consideration that I decided in September 1939 to postpone the publication of my book on the subject, which, under the title of *Danegeld : A Study of Financial Appeasement*, was actually in the hands of my publishers. I felt at the outbreak of the war that, although I may have to criticise the Government for current mistakes committed in the sphere in which I have specialised,

I ought to avoid any criticism for past errors. For deplorable as it was that short-sighted politicians and bankers should have pursued a policy that had unwittingly helped Germany in her rearmament, to attack that policy after the outbreak of the war would be crying over spilt milk. On the assumption that with the outbreak of the war the policy of appeasement came to an end I decided to withhold the publication of my book until after the war, when it would be possible to view pre-war appeasement in the perspective of history.

At the present stage, however, I now feel justified to change my mind and to proceed with the publication of a book against appeasement, on much broader lines than the one which I withheld in 1939. It is because of the growing evidence of a new wave of appeasement in the political as well as in the economic sphere. The methods of this new appeasement will be described, in the hope that the publication of a detailed account of the utter failure of appeasement in the past will be helpful towards enabling us to avoid falling into the same error in the future.

Several of those who before the war associated themselves with the policy of appeasement threw themselves wholeheartedly in the anti-appeasement camp on the outbreak of the war, or have rendered great services to the democratic cause by collaborating in the war effort. They have thus lived down their past error of judgment. It is with some reluctance that I quoted the names of some of these converts among the pre-war appeasers; in particular I was reluctant to criticise Mr. R. S. Hudson's pre-war policy of appeasement, seeing that since the war he has done good work in the various Government

offices he has held. It would have been impossible,
however, to write an account of pre-war appeasement
without criticising him and others in a similar position.
My object throughout this book was not to pillory
individuals but to denounce a policy which I consider harmful to the best interests of this country
and of mankind.

In itself the denunciation of past mistakes would
not be sufficient. It is necessary for us to produce
a constructive alternative. In the absence of such
alternative appeasers have a good chance of being
able to convince the British public that after the
coming victory Germany is bound to recover sooner
or later her former power, as she recovered it after
the victory of 1918. According to the appeasers the
choice lies between allowing her to retain her power
and thereby appeasing her and trying in vain to prevent her from recovering her power and thereby
antagonising her. Fortunately there is a third solution, and it is the object of this book to indicate the
method by which it is possible, in my opinion, to
prevent Germany from becoming once more a menace
to world freedom.

P. E.

London, *May* 1941
130 Queen's Gate, S.W.7

CONTENTS

xi

CHAPTER IX

CHAPTER X

CHAPTER XI

CHAPTER XII

CHAPTER XIII

CHAPTER XIV

CHAPTER XV

CHAPTER XVI

CHAPTER I

APPEASEMENT may be defined as the policy which aims at safeguarding peace by means of yielding to the unjustified demands, or satisfying the excessive requirements, of an aggressive Power under the pressure of threats, actual or implied. This aim may be pursued by making political concessions such as the surrender of territories, or by abstaining from preventing the conquest of territory belonging to a third country by an aggressive Power. It can also be pursued by means of concessions of an economic nature, in which case the policy is one of economic appeasement.

It is difficult to draw an exact borderline between political and economic appeasement. The ultimate aim of the aggressive Power consists of territorial aggrandisement for the sake of both political (or strategical) and economic advantages. Economic arguments are frequently resorted to in support of territorial claims which could not possibly be put forward on any other ground. Any expansion of territory achieved as a result of political appeasement tends to increase the economic resources of the aggressive Power through adding to its food and raw-material resources, its industrial capacity, its labour supply, and possibly also its gold reserves and foreign assets. On the other hand, any act of economic appeasement tends to strengthen the political and military position

1

of the aggressive Power and to increase its ability to enforce claims of a political nature.

The main arguments on which the policy of appeasement is based are as follows :

(1) It is resentment over what is regarded to be intolerable grievances (political or economic) that makes for an aggressive foreign policy.

(2) By conversion of "have not" nations into "have" nations — both in a political and economic sense — the cause of war would be eliminated.

(3) It would take some time before the aggressive Power could digest politically and economically its newly acquired territory and before it could be ready for its next move.

In the predominant majority of instances the claim that the aggressive Power is suffering under intolerable hardship is either entirely devoid of foundation or grossly exaggerated. It puts forward its claims simply because it feels strong enough to enforce them by acts of aggression or even by threats of aggression. The history of recent years has conclusively proved that even after the satisfaction of its genuine grievances the aggressive Power shows itself at least as much dissatisfied as before, and proceeds to work up new artificial grievances. It insists upon the full elimination of any minor hardships, even if this could only be done at the expense of inflicting a major hardship upon other countries.

The predominant majority of wars have not been caused by the existence of intolerable hardships, whether political or economic, but by a desire to inflict them upon other nations. What were the grievances which forced Louis XIV, Napoleon or Frederick the Great to commit acts of aggression ? Or, more recently, was Prussia driven by any gross injustice to attack Denmark, Austria and France between 1864 and 1870 ? In 1914 there were, it is true, intolerable grievances — on the part of the victims of the aggression, not on the part of the aggressor. Serbia was being strangled economically by Austria-Hungary. In spite of this she did not attack : she was attacked.

Nations are usually classified static and dynamic nations, or old and young nations, or " have " and " have not " nations. According to popular theory nations which are rich and old are static, while those which are poor and young are dynamic. Recent history provided, however, too many exceptions to this rule. The contention of some historians that the reason why Germany and Italy are aggressive is that their national unity is of recent origin is discredited by the fact that the first major act of aggression after the last war was committed by Japan, whose national unity is much older than that of any of the static nations in Europe. Again, that possession of additional national wealth and resources does not rule out an aggressive policy is shown by the example of Italy in 1936–39. What usually happens when a " have not " nation becomes a " have " nation is that it wants to have more and still more. After the conquest of Abyssinia, Mussolini declared that " From now on Italy has entered the ranks of the satisfied nations ". This did not prevent him from seeking the expansion of Italy's power through intervention in the Spanish civil war, or through conquering Albania and putting forward claims for Corsica, Nice and Tunis.

Germany's appetite has been growing with the absorption of each additional victim of her aggressive policy.

Whether a nation is static or dynamic depends not so much upon the size of the territories and resources it controls or the length of its history as a united nation as upon the fundamental character of its people or of its régime. Japan is dynamic because of the ultra-nationalistic character of her people and because, after many centuries of peaceful isolation, her military leaders developed the ambition of conquering Asia. Italy is dynamic because of the personal ambitions of the head of her present régime. In the case of Germany, however, the aggressively nationalistic character of the German people is combined with the aggressively expansionistic character of her present régime and the unlimited personal ambitions of her present ruler. This combination makes for the maximum degree of dynamism.

After the last war the British attitude towards dynamic States underwent a remarkable change. The superhuman exertions and sacrifices made during 1914–1918 resulted in a high degree of war-weariness. To begin with, this feeling was universal all over Europe, but the dynamic nations recovered from it much sooner than the static nations. Germany in particular soon reverted to her pre-1914 bellicosity. Her people resumed extolling the martial virtues at a time when in Great Britain anyone in favour of defensive rearmament was denounced as a warmonger and a hireling of war profiteers.

Germany was by far the largest beneficiary of the policy of appeasement. In her case the static nations began to make concessions long before they were forced to do so by any threat of aggression. The policy of a ruthless application of the Peace Treaty against her reached its climax with the occupation of the Ruhr. With the evacuation of the Ruhr and the conclusion of the Dawes scheme the static nations embarked upon a policy of progressive concessions. Many of Germany's grievances arising from the Treaty of Versailles were removed by means of such concessions even before the advent of Hitler. The Rhineland was evacuated after the conclusion of the Locarno Pact, long before the period prescribed by the Treaty of Versailles expired. Reparations payments were regulated by the Dawes Plan and subsequently by the Young Plan in such a way as to avoid disorganising Germany's economic and financial structure. Indeed, money for the payment of the Dawes and Young annuities was provided in reality by international financiers, and these same financiers also raised the funds for the replacement of capital destroyed in Germany during the advanced inflation of 1923. In 1931 reparations payments were temporarily suspended, while in the following year they were in practice abolished as a result of the Lausanne agreement. Long before Hitler assumed power there were no foreign troops left on German territory, nor was Germany under any obligation to pay tribute to the victorious Allies. The remaining grievances arising from the peace treaties were by no means intolerable, and judging by the progress made between 1924 and 1932 it was reasonable to assume that they too would be gradually eliminated by means of peaceful adjustment.

The German nation entirely failed to appreciate the concessions made voluntarily by the Allies. As and when the terms of the Versailles Treaty were relaxed

B

her spirit of aggressive nationalism strengthened. It was not until after the evacuation of the Rhineland that the National Socialist Party, which until then was but one of the numerous freak parties, became an important factor in German politics. And it was only after the abolition of reparations in 1932 that Hitler came to power.

While the National Socialist movement grew largely upon the misery of the middle classes, expropriated through the inflation of 1923, and of the working classes which suffered through the depression that followed the Wall Street slump of 1929, the major factor of its immense success was the revival of that aggressive nationalism which for some years after the defeat of 1918 suffered temporary eclipse. During the years while Germany was under the shadow of French bayonets this aggressive nationalism remained more or less repressed. Even then various nationalist movements made slow but steady progress. Their progress became accentuated when the German people realised that there was no longer any likelihood of a French invasion and that Germany could once more be openly nationalistic with impunity.

While National Socialism was the socialistic brand of nationalism, there was also the Stahlhelm movement which was the militaristic brand, and also the industrialists' nationalist movement as personified by Hugenberg, Thyssen, etc. Even in the absence of Hitler and of National Socialism Germany would have reverted to aggressive nationalism by about 1933, but certainly not later than 1934, when the internal troubles of France provided an excellent opportunity for putting the clock back to 1914. The régime of von Papen and General von Schleicher in 1932–1933

provided a foretaste of military and capitalist nationalism. In January 1933 the three brands of nationalism
combined forces, with the socialistic brand of nationalism gradually assuming control. Possibly in the
absence of the economic depression the nationalistic
trend in Germany would have remained military and
capitalistic in character. It would have. been none
the less aggressive.

The world-wide depression and the series of financial
crises between 1931 and 1938 played a very important
part in the development of German aggressive nationalism under Nazi rule, but in a totally different sense
from what is generally assumed. In their efforts to
balance their budgets amidst great difficulties Great
Britain and France weakened their national defences
at a time when Germany, disregarding orthodox
considerations, was spending milliards on rearmament.
In France in particular the perennial crisis of the
franc was accompanied by frequent changes of
Government and general internal political and social
instability. This provided the maximum of encouragement for Germany to violate the Treaty of Versailles.
She could do so with impunity because the French
Governments that followed each other in close suc-
cession were too much absorbed in their futile efforts
to bolster up the franc to concentrate their efforts
upon safeguarding the security of France.

During this period political appeasement reigned
supreme. Whenever Hitler abolished a clause of the
Treaty of Versailles by unilateral action there was an
outburst of indignation in the Press and Parliaments
of the Allied countries, but their Governments submitted to the *fait accompli* in each instance. Yet until
about 1937 it would have been easy for the Allies to

nip in the bud the menace of German aggressive
nationalism by means of a preventive war. Instead
they chose the slippery slope of appeasement. They
meekly submitted to the rearmament of Germany, to
the unilateral abolition of international régimes over
German inland waterways, and even to the reoccupa-
tion and remilitarisation of the Rhineland. In some
instances, however, the British and French Governments themselves made concessions in favour of
Germany in pursuance of their policy of appeasement.
There was, for instance, the restoration of the Saar
district to Germany. By virtue of the Treaty of
Versailles this could have been deferred for many
years by insisting that Germany should pay to France
in advance the purchase price of the Saar coalfields.
France would have been well within her Treaty rights
to adopt such an attitude, and at that time at any
rate she was strong enough to do so without running
any risk. Yet she willingly yielded to British pressure
and waived her claim for payment in advance, in
order to appease Hitler who declared that once the
Saar district was restored to Germany she would have
no longer any territorial claims against France.

Another characteristic act of political appeasement
was the Anglo-German naval agreement of 1935. It
is difficult to find justification from a British point
of view for the conclusion of this agreement, which
was a great diplomatic and moral victory for Germany.
The limitation placed upon Germany's naval power
by this treaty was of no practical significance since,
owing to the pace of her rearmament on the land and
in the air, she was in any case incapable of increasing
her sea power even to the limits prescribed by the
treaty. In any case it was obvious that the moment

she would be able to do so, Hitler would no longer feel himself bound by the limitations agreed upon.

The policy of political appeasement reached its culminating point in 1938 when the democratic Powers accepted the annexation of Austria and forced Czecho-Slovakia to surrender to Germany the Sudeten district. It was after the annexation of Austria that the appeaser school came forward with the argument that the acquisition of such a substantial territory by Germany would make for peace at any rate for some time to come, since it would take years for Germany to digest politically and economically her new acquisition. In less than six months the falsity of this argument was proved beyond the slightest doubt. Accordingly, after the acquisition of the Sudeten district few people expected Hitler to keep the peace for more than a few months.

The conquest of Czecho-Slovakia brought political appeasement to an end, but the policy of appeasement was continued in the economic and financial sphere. It was indeed the height of absurdity that while the democratic Powers were seeking to build up a system of alliances to resist Hitler, in the economic sphere Germany continued to benefit by concessions made in the interest of appeasement. By that time it must have been obvious that the only result of such concessions was to increase Germany's economic war potential and make it easier for her to prepare for her next act of aggression.

The explanation why at that stage the main sphere of activity of appeasement was diverted from the political to the economic sphere is simple. After the occupation of Austria and the Sudeten district, appeasers were no longer able to claim that Germany had intolerable political grievances. In particular, after the conquest of Prague such political grievances arising from the Treaty of Versailles as survived disappeared as compared with the political grievances inflicted upon Czecho-Slovakia by Germany. On the other hand, it was still possible to find people who believed that Germany had been suffering under intolerable economic grievances for lack of adequate foreign markets and raw-material resources.

Economic appeasement had, from the point of view of the appeasers, certain other advantages over political appeasement. For one thing it was less conspicuous and the economic sphere provided better scope for surreptitious appeasement than the political sphere. Any concession of a political nature was bound to receive the maximum of publicity. On the other hand, certain forms of economic appeasement could be carried out entirely in secret, and even when the facts leaked out the general public failed to take much interest in them. It was only in one or two instances that acts of economic appeasement aroused really widespread interest. This explains why it was possible to pursue economic appeasement until the eve of the war, long after the policy of political appeasement had been repudiated.

The outbreak of the war did not by any means bring the policy of appeasement to an end. Even though attempts at appeasing Germany came to a halt the policy continued in favour of friendly neutrals and unfriendly non-belligerents. In relation to Germany, too, appeasement was by no means dead, though for some months it appeared to be dormant. The movement now assumed a much more subtle form than before the war. Apart from a few fanatical pacifists nobody now openly suggests that Hitler should be offered concessions in order to bring the war to an end. Any open support of a policy of appeasing Germany in existing circumstances would provoke such a determined and sweeping opposition among the public that it would defeat its object. The Government itself is emphatically against the appeasement of Germany. On the other hand, appeasement has many influential supporters outside official quarters who are doing their utmost to influence the Government's policy by means of influencing public opinion.

Appeasers of all classes have changed their tactics. Instead of delivering a frontal attack as before the war upon the nation's determination to resist to the utmost, they now seek to sneak in by the back door. The device used is, however, largely identical with that of the pre-war appeasers. Their present aim is to " Runcimanise " British opinion. It will be remembered that during the Sudeten crisis of 1938 the will to support Czecho-Slovakia against German aggression was sapped by Lord Runciman's report stating that even if the democratic countries should win the war it would be necessary nevertheless to surrender to Germany the Sudeten districts because the German majority of their population is desirous of joining the Reich. This statement led to the widespread feeling that it would be utterly futile to fight a war with Germany if even in case of victory peace would have to be concluded on the basis of the German demands. The present wave of appeasement, too, aims at convincing the British public that even in case of a total victory over Germany she will have to be allowed to remain strong, united, powerful and prosperous, and that she will have to be allowed to retain at least economic control of the Continent, or at any rate of the countries in Eastern and South-Eastern Europe which she claims as her living space.

Should the appeasers succeed in inducing the British public to share their views this might easily lead to the conclusion that it would be utterly futile to fight this war to the bitter end, since in any case Germany would have to be granted terms which she might accept even without having been defeated. This method of insidious appeasement is much more dangerous than the pre-war method of open appeasement, because it appeals to the sentimental and humanitarian character of the British nation. Those who for humanitarian reasons are engaged in agitating in favour of letting Germany off lightly after her defeat are blissfully oblivious of the fact that they are engaged in actively supporting the policy of appeasement pursued by Ribbentrop's British friends. The latter, who were very much in evidence during the years that preceded the war, now prefer on the whole to remain in the background. It was only quite recently that, following upon the publication of Lord Vansittart's highly challenging pamphlet, some of them ventured to come out into the open.

This new movement of appeasement is worked in the economic sphere perhaps to an even larger degree than was pre-war appeasement. While most appeasers pay lip-service to the necessity of a curtailment of Germany's expansionary political ambitions, they are in favour of satisfying her expansionary economic ambitions.

It would indeed be difficult to exaggerate the dangers of this new wave of appeasement from the point of view of the Allied cause. Not only does it tend to undermine the determination to fight on until total victory is achieved, but it also tends to weaken our war effort. Experience has shown that hatred of an enemy is a powerful incentive to work harder in the interests of victory, and it would be foolish to allow appeasers to destroy this factor. Moreover, the adoption of a policy of appeasement in this country would be strongly disapproved of by the Allied nations and would inevitably weaken the resistance of the population of conquered territories. As it is there is a widespread suspicion amongst them that after victory Great Britain will be only too ready to forgive and forget once more, and will leave the Continental nations at the mercy of a strong and powerful Germany. And so long as this is believed there is little inducement for the oppressed peoples to risk their lives by committing acts of sabotage or even to suffer disadvantages by refusing to collaborate in Germany's economic war effort. For this reason alone it is of vital importance from the point of view of the victory of the democratic cause that nothing should be said or done which would encourage the feeling that after the war official British policy would relapse into appeasement.

Curiously enough, while pre-war appeasement was the subject of heated attacks, appeasement during the war and the preparation of a policy of appeasement for after the war escaped attention almost completely. Indeed, the very existence of the revival of appeasement in a new form is ignored by most people, including many of those who participate in the movement and who are completely unaware of the fact that in trying to demobilise hatred against Germany and to secure generous peace terms for her they have joined the current in favour of appeasement. The sooner they and the public in general realise the mischievous character of this new wave of appeasement, the better it will be from the point of view of the democratic cause.

CHAPTER II

THE policy of appeasement pursued in the democratic countries before this war was largely the result of circumstances of a general nature. In France the endless series of internal financial and political troubles between 1932 and 1938 was largely responsible for the reluctance of the country and its leaders to face with determination the growing menace of German aggression. In Great Britain war-weariness combined with financial orthodoxy made for appeasement. At the same time, however, the importance of the personal factor should not be underestimated.

In Great Britain in particular the policy of appeasement was largely the consequence of weakness of leadership. Moreover, the Government before the war had been subject to a growing pressure on the part of a small but extremely influential clique. Even though Ribbentrop failed in his mission to bring about an Anglo-German alliance, which would have suited Hitler's immediate purpose, he certainly succeeded in gathering round him a set of politicians, society men and women, bankers, industrialists and newspapermen who threw themselves wholeheartedly in support of the policy of appeasement. The activities of the various groups of appeasers were described and denounced innumerable times in the contemporary Press. Some of these accounts about the " Cliveden Set " and other pro-Nazi or pro-German circles may

15

have been exaggerated. Nevertheless, in substance it is true that there was constant pressure upon the Government on the part of influential politicians, formidable society hostesses, powerful newspaper editors and proprietors in favour of continuing their policy of political appeasement.

The camp of appeasers was a very mixed company indeed. It included those who had become converted in favour of Fascist and Nazi doctrines; the pro-German and anti-French elements; those who felt that in the past Great Britain's attitude had been by no means above reproach; those who regarded Hitler as a bulwark against Communism; bankers and business men anxious to retain their profit on trade with Germany; non-resister pacifists who would have preferred slavery under Hitler to a war; isolationists of various kinds; wishful thinkers who succeeded in persuading themselves that Hitler's latest demand was positively the last and its satisfaction would dispose of the danger of aggression; and a number of cowards pure and simple who would have conceded Hitler anything rather than risk their very, very precious skins.

Adherents to the British Union of Fascists and other minor organisations of a more or less similar character adopted a policy of appeasement partly because of their sympathy towards Nazi doctrines and partly because they hoped to increase their membership by attracting all those who were against war. While it is easy to understand their political opportunism, it is difficult to follow the logic of their pro-German attitude on the ground of the identity of their political philosophy with that of Nazi Germany and Fascist Italy. That Communists all over the world blindly

obey the instructions from Moscow is understandable.
After all, Communism is, in theory at any rate, internationalist. On the other hand, Nazi-ism and Fascism
are essentially nationalist movements. Their declared
aim is to expand and build up· vast empires at the
expense of existing empires. This being so, it is
difficult to understand why British Fascists should
look to Berlin in the same way as British Communists
look to Moscow, or Roman Catholics all over the
world look to the Vatican City. The mere fact
that British Fascists believe that Fascism is a highly
efficient system worth imitating is in itself no reason
why they should support a foreign policy favouring
the countries where Fascism operates. After all, both
Germany and Italy were dynamic nations and it was
obvious that their claims could only be satisfied largely
at the expense of the British Empire. In the circumstances every British nationalist, whether or not he
is a Fascist, was bound to see that sooner or later
there would be a clash between Great Britain on the
one hand and the two Fascist States on the other.
It would have been understandable if the British
Fascists had confined themselves to urging the
Government and the British public to emulate the
highly efficient economic system which operated with
such conspicuous success in Germany and Italy, in
order to be able to resist the German-Italian onslaught
when it should come. It is much less understandable
why the British Fascists should have adopted an
attitude of " love thy enemies if they are efficient ".

A much more dangerous section of the appeasement
camp was that of the pro-Germans. Hereditary
influences account largely for the prevalence of pro-
German and anti-French feelings among a large number

of Englishmen. After all, rivalry between Great
Britain and Germany only began to develop towards
the close of the nineteenth century and appeared to
have come to an end with the scuttling of the German
Fleet at Scapa Flow in 1919. On the other hand,
from the Norman invasion in 1066 until the collapse
of the Second French Empire in 1871, France had
always been regarded as the hereditary foe. Even in
more recent times anti-French feeling flared up at the
Fashoda incident in 1898 and also during the early
years that followed the last war when it was feared
in England that German militarism had been replaced
by French militarism. Thus, while anti-German
feeling in Great Britain existed on a large scale for a
bare twenty years before the last war and some six
years before this war, anti-French feeling looks back
upon a past covering nearly nine hundred years, with
very few interruptions. Even during the present war,
amidst the worst period of the Blitzkrieg, a Labour
M.P. had the audacity to declare in the House of
Commons that after all Germany had been this
country's hereditary friend.

Apart from this influence, which in the majority
of instances worked subconsciously, many appeasers
were pro-Germans for a variety of sentimental or
practical reasons. During the years of peace hundreds
of thousands of British tourists paid visits to Germany,
and almost without exception they came back with
favourable impressions. Even at a time when tension
between the two countries was approaching its climax
the German Customs officials and other officials with
whom British tourists had dealings were under strict
instructions to be polite and friendly, which is more
than French Customs officials could say for themselves

at the best of times. Most people are easily influenced
in their political attitude by trivial experiences, and
the Germans knew how to take advantage of this.
Every British tourist who was addressed in broken
English by a smiling German Customs official, or
who met nice Germans during his stay in the Black
Forest, became a potential appeaser. Having had such
pleasant recollections of the Germans he met, he refused
to believe that the German nation could be really
as aggressive as it was accused of being. Yet the
contrast between the personal charm of individual
Germans and the brutality of the German nation as a
nation can easily be explained. For one thing, the
predominant majority of British tourists visited the
Rhineland or Southern Germany and not Prussia
proper. What is even more important, the behaviour
of a crowd or of a nation is totally different from the
behaviour of the individuals of whom it consists. An
aggressive minority can easily sway a crowd or a
nation in the direction of brutality, for the majority
either swims with the tide or remains passive.

Yet another section of appeasers belongs to what
we may describe as the *mea culpa* school. After each
new dishonourable act on the part of Hitler and his
Germans these appeasers were at once ready to con-
done the offence on the ground that, after all, we too
in the past were culpable of similar offences. In
excuse of the untold horrors of the concentration camp
they recall the not altogether genteel methods
employed in England in the reign of Henry VIII or
Queen Elizabeth. It does not occur to them that
mankind has made some progress since the sixteenth
century and that standards of conduct of nations as
of individuals have changed. As an excuse for the

various acts of aggression committed by Hitler they readily quote the British act of aggression against the Transvaal at the end of the last century. What they omit is that after the complete conquest of the Boers their freedom was completely restored. Not only were they not kept oppressed by their conquerors, but they were even allowed to oppress in a sense the very substantial British minority. However, logic is not exactly the strong suit of Hitler's British apologists, who readily provide material for Goebbels in denouncing their country's past offences, real or imaginary.

One of the favourite trump cards of the *mea culpa* school is to recall the atrocities committed in Ireland both in past centuries and, more recently, during the early years that followed the last war. As far as the recent atrocities were concerned, it ought to be borne in mind that they were committed during a period of acute civil war. It is easy to imagine what would happen if the population of any of the countries conquered by Germany committed one-tenth of the acts of violence committed by the Sinn Feiners during that period against the British Army and British civilian residents in Ireland. In Poland any isolated act of violence is avenged through the mass execution of Polish hostages. Had the British been as cruel as the Germans, the population of Ireland would have been exterminated completely long ago. Rather than proceed with the distasteful reprisals the British people preferred to relinquish its control over Eire.

At the other extreme there are the old-fashioned Imperialists who have turned appeasers simply because they considered Stalin as a greater menace to the British Empire than Hitler. This group of appeasers was heavily represented among the nobility

and the ruling classes in general. Their attitude
might have been understandable in the 'twenties when
during the early post-war disturbances, and especially
during the General Strike of 1926, the bogy of Communism appeared to assume reality. By the late
'thirties, however, it was obvious that in the absence
of a major upheaval such as a world war there was
not the slightest chance for a world revolution. In
particular in Great Britain there was no reason whatever to suppose that Communism would ever assume
power. In France Communists represented a very
appreciable section of the population ; in Germany,
too, before the advent of Hitler they constituted a
major factor in German politics. In Great Britain,
on the other hand, the election results indicated that
Communism was a *quantité négligeable* and certainly
was not a factor which should have influenced the
attitude of the wealthy classes in major matters of
foreign policy. But then, when these people spoke
about the Communist menace they used the term in
the broadest sense. It covered the tyranny of trade
unionism, the risk of a return of the Labour Government with a clear majority at the next election, and
perhaps even the " socialistic " tendencies of progressive Conservatives who sought to minimise that
risk by stealing the thunder of the Labour Party.
Some industrialists, bankers and members of old
families regarded Hitler with approval because he
imprisoned the Communists and wrecked the trade
unions in Germany. What these people failed to
realise was that at the same time Hitler also broke
the power of their opposite numbers in Germany, the
Junkers, and reduced the power of captains of industry
until they became hardly more than paid managers in

their own works. They refused to see that, generally speaking, the former ruling classes in Germany were the chief victims of the advent of National Socialism. While the rank and file of Socialists and Communists joined the Nazis, the members of the *Herrenklub* and heavy industrialists of the Thyssen type stood aside sulking and cursing their own folly for having been instrumental to Hitler's advent to power. The blindness of the British ruling classes in this respect is all the stranger since they had ample opportunity to ascertain from their friends in Germany how the latter felt about Hitler. The catchword that he was a bulwark against Communism was stronger than the wealth of evidence showing that he actually brought Communism to the Rhine — the nationalist brand of Communism it is true, as distinct from the internationalist brand of Moscow, but Communism nevertheless.

Those who drank Ribbentrop's champagne chose to ignore such considerations. They dreamt of an Anglo-German alliance against Soviet Russia, and mobilised all their influence to improve Anglo-German relations. They provided the maximum of encouragement for Hitler to go ahead with his aggressive foreign policy by assuring Ribbentrop that they would be able to prevent the Government from taking a firm stand against Germany. This at a time when in the absence of such assurances Hitler might not have felt safe to run the risk of antagonising Great Britain.

There were among the appeasers a number of important bankers and business men who were in favour of a policy of *rapprochement* with Germany for purely selfish business considerations. Their firms were doing profitable business with Germany and they were in favour of a policy that made such transactions possible. The fact that their activities assisted Germany in her rearmament failed to influence their attitude. There were other pro-German bankers and business men whose motives were less sordid. They were simply pro-German because of their vague fears that another war, no matter what its outcome, would bring Socialism to Great Britain. For this reason they were in favour of avoiding another war at no matter what cost.

The blindness of these Right Wing appeasers was only equalled by that of the Left Wing appeasers, who seriously imagined that, by means of a policy of pacifism and non-resistance, it would be possible to avoid war. Some of the pacifists went so far as to prefer a bloodless conquest by Hitler to armed resistance. It became fashionable among intellectuals of the Aldous Huxley type to preach the practical advantages of passive resistance, as a result of which they thought conquerors could be made to realise that conquests did not pay in the long run. They quoted historical examples to show that on occasions conquerors decided to give up their ill-gotten gains as a result of such persistent passive resistance. What these people refused to realise is that a conqueror who is entirely devoid of human feelings is quite capable of bringing passive resistance to an end with the aid of terrorising methods so successfully applied within Germany.

Other appeasers of the George Lansbury type started from the assumption that, after all, even dictators are human beings (" Even Hitler had a Mother " was a fashionable song in those days) and that their better nature could be made to prevail if

approached in the right way. Accordingly Mr. Lansbury set out to pay a visit to Hitler and Mussolini
and was duly impressed by the friendly reception he
had. Indeed, the dictators had every reason to display
friendliness towards him for, after all, he served the
cause of appeasement so helpful to their designs. Just
as the British industrialists refused to realise that their
German opposite numbers were anything but happy
under the Nazi régime, so British pacifists chose to
ignore the fact that pacifists in Germany were sent to
concentration camps. They continued in their unilateral efforts at appeasement, solemnly believing that
if they refused to be attacked there could be no war.

There was also a small but influential group which
held the view that Great Britain should disinterest
herself altogether in the affairs of the Continent and
should isolate herself from European affairs, relying
upon the protective strength of the Royal Navy.
The isolationists believed that once Germany's ambitions on the Continent were satisfied she would be quite
willing to share world power with Great Britain,
leaving in the latter's hands the control of the seas.
Yet the growing German demand for the restoration
of colonies and for a radical redistribution of colonial
possessions should have made it obvious that Germany's
ambitions were by no means confined to the European
continent. The isolationists chose to ignore this as
they chose to ignore the fact that, by gaining possession
of the Atlantic coast of Europe and of the shipyards
of western and northern European countries, Germany's potential striking power against Great Britain
would increase immensely.

Perhaps the most numerous section in the camp
of appeasers was that of the wishful thinkers who until

the very eve of the war refused to believe that Hitler
really meant war. After each arbitrary act Hitler
declared that this was positively his last arbitrary act ;
that henceforth all changes would be made through
negotiations ; and that Germany's territorial claims
had now been satisfied. Even though he broke his
word again and again, every time he made a fresh
promise there were millions of people in Great Britain
who chose to believe him. They refused to face reality
because reality was too horrible. They preferred to
deceive themselves into believing that this time Hitler
really meant what he said, or at any rate they were
all in favour of giving him another and yet another
chance to prove that this time he meant to keep his
word.

There is reason to believe that Mr. Chamberlain
and his political supporters belonged to this group
of appeasers. While the fact that Great Britain was
not adequately prepared may have influenced the
attitude of those holding responsible positions during
1938, in previous years it was wishful thinking on the
part of the Government that was responsible for the
slackness of the British rearmament efforts. Lord
Baldwin, and after him Mr. Chamberlain, did not wish
to disorganise the peaceful routine of the British
nation because they did not expect Hitler to go beyond
a certain point in his aggressive foreign policy. Perhaps they had not read *Mein Kampf*, or if they had
they refused to believe it. Hitler succeeded during
the early years of his régime in making his opponents
underrate him.

The factor of physical fear assumed predominant
importance in the movement of appeasement at the
time of the Czecho-Slovak crisis of September 1938.

The distribution of gas-masks made the wide sections of the public realise the imminence and probable horrors of war. Until then most people considered it simply inconceivable that during the lifetime of the same generation there should be two world wars. The sudden realisation that a flood of unprecedented horrors might break loose upon them at any moment constituted a very severe test for the physical courage of the millions. Many of them were not in a position to realise the broader implications of the position. They simply wanted to avoid at all costs being plunged into a war. In September 1938 moral rearmament was even less advanced than physical rearmament. The extent to which the fear factor was responsible for the wave of appeasement that swept the country was only realised after the danger was over. The undisguised relief displayed by the House of Commons when Mr. Chamberlain announced his invitation to Munich and the mass hysteria displayed by the crowds at Croydon and around Downing Street on his return from Munich after having become a party to one of the most inglorious acts ever committed by a British statesman, showed that his attitude was endorsed by a very large section of the British nation. That very same crowd of Londoners which two years later withstood so splendidly the horrors of the Blitzkrieg enthusiastically welcomed Mr. Chamberlain's surrender to Hitler because it appeared to mean peace, if not in our time, at any rate for the next six months.

Let us take things as they are. Even those of us who strongly disapproved of the Munich surrender because we fully realised its consequences were trembling in our boots during the crisis when thinking of the horrible consequences of a firm attitude on the

part of this country. Those millions who were not
in a position to realise what Czecho-Slovakia meant
can hardly be blamed for allowing their fear of war to
influence their judgment. It is to their credit that
while it appeared that Mr. Chamberlain would take
up a firm stand they refrained from any manifestation
of their fear. The complete absence of anti-war
demonstrations during September 1938 can only be
appreciated in the light of the subsequent hysterical
scenes when it became known that the war was off
for the time being. Even so, although there were no
outward manifestations of the fear of war, the camp
of appeasers was fully aware of its existence and took
advantage of it before, during and after the Czecho-
Slovak crisis. Their ranks became swollen by the
adherence of those who, under the influence of physical
fear, were prepared to concede Hitler anything to
avoid having to risk their life and property in defence
of their country and of democracy.

Throughout these years Europe was driven helplessly towards her doom. It did not require an unusual
degree of prophetic foresight to realise at any time
from 1936 onwards, if not before, that another world
war was a mere question of time. Considering that
this was very obvious to any student of politics, there
is no excuse for the lack of judgment on the part of
the various schools of appeasers. Nor can their claim
that their policy at least postponed the inevitable be
accepted in mitigation of their gross error of judgment.
For one thing, it is by no means certain that a firm
stand against Hitler would have accelerated the war.
What is certain is that Hitler made better use of the
time gained than his opponents. Up to the very eve
of the war rearmament in Great Britain and in the

democratic countries was proceeding at a very leisurely
pace, while it was proceeding at full speed in Germany.
To those who maintain that in September 1938 the
Air Force and anti-aircraft defences of Great Britain
were grossly inadequate, the answer is that during
the twelve months between the Czecho-Slovak crisis
and the war the increase of the German Air Force was
incomparably larger than that of the Allied Air
Forces. While in 1938 Germany would have had to
cope with the highly efficient defences of Czecho-
Slovakia, by 1939 the vast mass of war material which
a year earlier would have been used against her was
in her possession. During the twelve months gained
through the Munich surrender the British Army did
not increase to any appreciable extent owing to the
delay in the introduction of conscription and the
establishment of a Ministry of Supply. On the other
hand, the Germans were able to establish, train and
equip many dozens of new divisions. In September
1938 the Siegfried Line was in a half-finished state
and was not adequately equipped with guns. It was
after the Czecho-Slovak surrender that the guns which
would have served to resist the German invasion of
Czecho-Slovakia were transferred to the Siegfried
Line. The chances are that while London and other
British cities would have got a worse pounding in
1938 than they got in 1940, the superiority of the
French forces over the German forces, divided between
the Siegfried Line and the Czecho-Slovak border,
would have been decisive. Over and above all, at
that time it would have been possible to obtain the
active collaboration of Soviet Russia. The loss of her
support and the failure to make full use of the respite
gained through the policy of appeasement aggravate

the charges for which the appeasers will have to answer before the judgment of history.

After the outbreak of the war the appeasers lay low for a while, though their surreptitious activities in favour of a peace by compromise never ceased altogether. Lord Vansittart's broadcast and pamphlet on Germany's *Black Record* brought them to the surface, and it seems that the participants in the new campaign of appeasement which has been developed for some time are largely identical with the supporters of pre-war appeasement. While, in many instances, pre-war appeasers realised their mistake and either changed their policy or at any rate abstained from any further efforts, it is safe to say that a very large section of both Right Wing and Left Wing appeasers is now as active as before the war.

CHAPTER III

THE FATAL MISTAKE OF VERSAILLES

ONE of the strongest weapons in the armoury of
appeasers is the claim that Germany had been un-
justly treated at Versailles. For many years Hitler
owed his popularity before German audiences largely
to the violence of his language when denouncing that
treaty. This fact is quoted by appeasers as a proof
that the advent of Hitler was really the fault of the
Allied statesmen responsible for the Treaty of Versailles.

A close examination of the argument in the light
of subsequent events shows that the resentment of
the German nation for the terms imposed upon her
by the victors was grossly exaggerated. Possibly
until 1939 the argument may have carried weight.
But then at that time the world did not realise what
kind of peace treaties Germany is capable of imposing
upon her opponents after their defeat or surrender.
It is true the treaties of Bucharest and Brest-Litovsk
during the last war gave a foretaste of things to come.
Even these treaties, however, drastic as they were
in comparison with the Treaty of Versailles, were
mildness itself in comparison with the peace imposed
upon Czecho-Slovakia, Poland and all the other
countries that came under German control from 1939
onwards.

Considering that Germany was responsible for the
war of 1914, that this war was fought for more than

four years with the utmost bitterness and at the cost
of ghastly sacrifices for the victorious nations, and
that their victory over Germany in 1918 was as complete as it was hard-earned, the Versailles "Diktat"
— to use one of Hitler's pet phrases — was very moderate. Indeed it is possible to claim that Germany's
appeasement began with the peace conference of
Paris. In an effort to conciliate the German nation
the statesmen of Versailles rejected the proposals
which might have safeguarded peace. Proposals for
the dismemberment of the Reich were rejected ; and
the result of the Treaty of Versailles was a considerable strengthening of Germany's internal political
unity through the removal of the various dynasties
which had been the principal obstacles to complete
unification. The peace conference rejected Marshal
Foch's demand for a permanent occupation of the
left bank of the Rhine and of the bridgeheads of the
right bank. Indeed the territorial losses inflicted upon
Germany after her defeat represented only a fraction
of her total territory. For the most part they were
inhabited by alien races. The number of people of
German race who came under non-German rule as
a result of the peace treaty represented a negligible
fraction of the total German population.

Germany, on the other hand, incorporated completely the nations which she defeated or which chose
to surrender. They simply disappeared from the map
of Europe as independent nations. Their populations
became subject races within the German *Machtgebiet*.
In comparison with these outrageous injustices the
minor injustices committed by those responsible for
drafting the frontiers of the Reich after the last war
disappeared in significance. Unless we accept Hitler's

axiom that anything that is to the interest of the German nation is a matter of supreme justice while anything that is contrary to its interest is unjust, we must admit in the light of subsequent experience that, comparatively speaking, the statesmen of Versailles exercised a remarkable degree of self-restraint in order to secure justice for the German people.

Admittedly, the reparations imposed upon Germany at Versailles and in subsequent agreements appeared to be unduly harsh. They were obviously beyond Germany's capacity of transferring payments through normal and recognised commercial and financial channels of transfer. The result, however, was simply that Germany re-borrowed abroad the whole amount paid in reparations, so that in practice she made no payments. In this respect, too, the difference between the Allied methods of exacting reparations from Germany and the German methods of exacting reparations from her defeated foes is very striking indeed. The Allies simply left it to Germany to raise the amounts she had to pay in reparations the best way she could. In fact the Allied Governments themselves helped her to raise part of the necessary amount through making arrangements for the issue of the Dawes and Young loans. Germany had been left in possession of her substantial gold reserve. While German assets in this country had been seized and their proceeds had been employed for the purposes of reparations, no efforts had been made to compel the German Government to surrender the assets of German nationals in former neutral countries. Apart from isolated instances during the French occupation of the Ruhr, German stocks of raw materials and other goods were not touched by the

Allied occupation armies, and in any case by far the greater part of Germany was spared Allied occupation.

The result of the gentlemanly methods of collecting reparations was that in practice no reparations were collected. As and when Germany discharged her political indebtedness to her former opponents she increased her commercial indebtedness abroad. And when it came to the final reckoning this commercial indebtedness was defaulted upon. Consequently it is true to say that the German nation paid no reparations to the Allies. Admittedly, taxes were collected from Germans by the Government of the Reich for the purpose of providing the reichsmarks paid into the reparations account controlled by the Agent-General of Reparations. On the other hand, German State Governments, municipalities and corporations were borrowing at the same time much larger amounts in New York, London, Amsterdam and Zurich for the purpose of erecting palatial municipal swimming baths, model workmen's dwellings, highly rationalised factories with most up-to-date equipment, etc.

Thus on balance Germany's national wealth increased as a net result of her financial operations with foreign countries. Had the reichsmarks collected in taxation for the requirements of reparations been spent on these municipal swimming baths, etc., instead of paying reparations and re-borrowing abroad the amounts paid, the result would have been less favourable for the German nation. Thus, paradoxical as it may sound, the Germans actually benefited by the system of reparations because it was linked up with the system of international borrowing. No part of the national production of Germany had to be diverted from German consumers in order to satisfy Allied reparations claims. The statement, repeated to boredom, that under the system of Versailles the German people was condemned to slavery for years in order to pay reparations was one of the outstanding lies of German propaganda. The victorious Allies left the German people in full possession of its national assets and of the fruits of its labour.

In contrast to this extremely lenient method of collecting reparations, the German conqueror from 1939 onwards devised much more ruthless methods. From the very first day of the occupation of the various countries Germany imposed upon her victims reparations under the name of occupation costs. In the case of France the amount was fixed at 400 million francs a day, even though the actual cost of the occupation was only estimated at 125 million francs. The difference was reparations pure and simple. With the aid of the proceeds of these payments Germany made large purchases in the occupied countries. In addition vast stocks of raw materials and foodstuffs were simply requisitioned without any pretence of compensation, while additional quantities were bought up through the working of clearing accounts and were paid for in the form of frozen reichsmark clearing balances.

Within a few months after their conquest the countries which were defeated by Germany or which surrendered to her were bled white as a result of the German method of collecting reparations. These reparations were collected partly in the form of the seizure of the gold reserves of Central Banks in so far as they were within the reach of the German invaders. Private holders of gold, foreign notes and foreign securities were also forced to surrender their holdings. For months the rolling stock of the railways of the conquered countries was used mainly for the purpose of removing vast quantities of loot, including raw materials and foodstuffs, factory equipments, art treasures stolen from private collections and even from museums, valuable stocks of vintage wines, and farm products or manufactured goods, purchased by the German troops or civilian invaders and paid for with notes specially printed for the benefit of the conquered peoples.

While the Allies were satisfied with book entries and purely fictitious transfers of payment, Germany collected her reparations in the form of goods with intrinsic value. While the net result of the reparations set up by the Treaty of Versailles was an increase of Germany's actual wealth, the obvious result of reparations payments to Germany from 1939 onwards was a rapid decline in the national wealth of the conquered peoples.

In the light of the experience of 1939–1941 it is now obvious that the reparations system imposed on Germany by the peace treaty, which was so often denounced as being ruthless and inhuman, was in reality as mild as it was ineffective. Whatever the intentions of the Allied statesmen may have been, in practice the result of their collective wisdom at Versailles was that Germany was let off reparations completely. This was simply because most countries were not prepared to increase their imports of German goods, and consequently there could be no genuine transfer of reparations payments. Germany, on the other hand, is quite willing to accept reparations in the form of goods. Indeed, she compels the conquered peoples to pay in that form.

Admittedly, Germany suffered disadvantages through the reparations system of Versailles, but not until that system broke down as a result of the international economic depression. The ill-conceived method of reparations was one of the main factors which led to the accumulation of a huge floating international indebtedness, the existence of which increased the vulnerability of the international financial structure. When as a result of the Wall Street slump and the subsequent economic depression an international financial crisis developed, the high degree of its intensity was therefore largely the consequence of the system of reparations. But, then, Germany was by no means the only country to suffer through this indirect effect of the Versailles system. Great Britain, too, suffered heavily under it, and the United States was one of its principal victims.

Moreover, to the extent to which the Versailles Treaty contributed to the international financial crises in 1931 and in subsequent years, it did so not because Germany was made to pay reparations but because in reality she was *not* made to pay reparations. Had the Allies in 1919 adopted the ruthlessly efficient methods of collecting reparations which Germany adopted twenty years later, these operations would have impoverished Germany but they would not have led to the accumulation of that international floating indebtedness which caused so much trouble in 1931. It was because the Allies chose an ineffective way of collecting reparations, by which Germany paid them with the aid of borrowed money without any loss to herself, that the financial upheaval which affected the whole world had arisen.

Admittedly, at least some of the statesmen responsible for the system of Versailles envisaged reparations as an indirect means of securing domination over Germany. Nobody with any sense of reality could possibly have expected Germany to make large genuine reparations payments under the then prevailing system. It is reasonable to assume that French statesmen such as M. Clemenceau or M. Poincaré were fully aware of the impossibility for Germany to make such payments unless she re-borrowed the whole or the larger part of the amounts imposed upon her. Nevertheless, they were hoping that a breakdown of the reparations system would provide an opportunity for France to interfere with Germany even to the extent of invading her. It was in fact a default on reparations payments that served as an excuse for France to occupy the Ruhr in 1923. After the liquidation of that unfortunate adventure, however, the reparations policy of the Allies definitely aimed at enabling Germany to convert her political indebtedness gradually into a commercial indebtedness. The Allies actually assisted Germany in re-organising her financial system in order to be able to re-borrow abroad the annuities payable under the Dawes scheme.

In 1924 France virtually agreed to relinquish her right to interfere with Germany on account of the default on reparations. The system of reparations was no longer used by France for political purposes but solely for financial purposes. In order to enable Germany to re-borrow the amounts payable to the Allies the latter had to restore her external credit partly through helping her to consolidate her finances and partly through indicating that inability to pay reparations would not lead to a recurrence of the

D

Ruhr occupation. Such a safeguard was implied in the Dawes scheme, even though France never formally relinquished her right to apply sanctions.

Needless to say it ought to have been obvious to everybody concerned that the system by which Germany was piling up external debts was essentially unsound and that it could not continue for ever. Year after year her interest charges on her external loans were mounting up and part of her new borrowings served the purpose of meeting these charges. There was, over and above all, the reparations claim of the Allies which, in theory at any rate, enjoyed priority over Germany's commercial indebtedness.

Evidently sooner or later this system was bound to break down. During 1926 and 1927 I repeatedly pointed out in the columns of the *Financial News* that it was essentially unsound to lend to Germany in the prevailing circumstances. In the absence of any new loans to her the situation would clear up and the world would know how much genuine reparations she would be capable of paying, while as a result of the re-borrowing of the amounts paid to the Allies the world continued to live in a fools' paradise. I was then given to understand that Whitehall viewed with disfavour my agitation, since it suited the Treasury's purpose that Germany should continue to make payments under the Dawes scheme with the aid of money borrowed from abroad. Any cessation of foreign lending to Germany would bring near the day of reckoning which the Treasury wanted to postpone as long as possible, even though it was obvious that it was bound to come sooner or later.

The day of reckoning did come in 1931 when foreign lending to Germany was suspended. Had it come a few years earlier the inverted pyramid of the international floating indebtedness would not have assumed such gigantic proportions and the crisis would in all probability have been milder.

From the foregoing it is evident that the system by which Germany paid reparations at the expense of her foreign creditors was proceeding with the knowledge and approval of the British authorities. They were fully aware that Germany was not paying any reparations in the real sense of the term. Nevertheless, they were anxious to uphold the fiction for fear that a breakdown in the system might lead to another French occupation of the Ruhr. They were presumably hoping that by gaining time they would reduce the likelihood of such developments when the breakdown eventually took place. The policy of Whitehall was thus inspired by a spirit of appeasement, in that it was anxious to avoid developments which might lead to French occupation of vital German territories. This method of appeasement succeeded in preventing France from satisfying her desire for security in the form of occupying the left bank of the Rhine under the excuse of Germany's default on reparations payments.

The British method of protecting Germany against France at the cost of eventually disorganising the international financial system met with absolutely no appreciation in Germany. It is one of the characteristic features of all experience in appeasement that Germany took for granted every concession and sacrifice made to her and showed no appreciation, let alone gratitude, for favours received. The facts that Germany paid in reality no reparations were skilfully disguised from the German public, which was fed on anti-Versailles propaganda mainly on the basis of the staggering figures of fictitious reparations payments. Hitler was by no means alone in misleading the German public into believing that they had been reduced to slavery by the reparations imposed upon them by the wicked Allies. Practically all politicians, economists and journalists in Germany between the two wars were unanimous in their denunciation of the reparations system, even after the default upon the German commercial indebtedness abroad made it obvious that in reality it was Germany's foreign creditors who were made to pay reparations.

The system of self-deception on the part of the Allies provided opportunity for Hitler and other demagogues to denounce wicked international financiers for enslaving Germany by imposing upon her heavy payments. Admittedly, the interest charged on long-term loans to Germany was rather high — it varied between 5 per cent and 7 per cent — though in the light of subsequent events it was evidently not nearly high enough to compensate lenders for the risk taken. The Germans, however, had no reason to complain since they re-borrowed abroad year after year the amounts they had to pay in interest, so that these payments as those of reparations annuities were also purely fictitious. This did not prevent Hitler from representing the growing burden of interest payments on external indebtedness as a gross injustice against Germany. Even when after 1931 interest payments were reduced to a negligible fraction of the amounts fixed in the loan contracts, and when capital repayments were stopped altogether, Hitler and his propagandists continued to denounce international financiers, although these financiers and their clients were the real victims of the Versailles system of reparations.

It is thus obviously a myth that Germany was exploited and impoverished and enslaved as a result of reparations. It was most unfortunate that the statesmen of Versailles should have devised a method which without securing the required results in favour of the Allies, and without imposing the slightest hardship upon their defeated foe in the long run, gave the latter material for working up a major grievance. Moreover, the imposition of fictitious reparations upon Germany to an amount running into astronomical figures gave rise to world-wide sympathy towards her. The existence of this fictitious burden concealed from most foreign observers the fact that, notwithstanding her defeat and temporary eclipse as a military power, she remained in the long run the most powerful country on the Continent and a permanent threat to peace in Europe. The sight of a Germany burdened with huge reparations inspired sentiments, in Great Britain, the United States and elsewhere, in favour of assisting the " unfortunate " people.

The British attitude in face of the Treaty of Versailles is worth studying, for the lessons of the past might be useful for the future. The ink on the signatures of the treaty was barely dry when a sweeping agitation developed against it. Mr. Keynes's *Economic Consequences of the Peace* was read more widely than any other book on economic subjects before or since. His denunciation of the reparations clauses of that treaty was based mainly on the well-founded fear that large reparations payments imposed upon Germany would disorganise the international commercial and financial system. His fears, which were amply confirmed by subsequent events, were shared by the City and by the international financial community in general. It is a fact which is only too easily forgotten that between 1919 and 1931 international financiers, Jewish or otherwise, were among the strongest supporters of a drastic revision of the Versailles Treaty for the benefit of Germany. Like Mr. Keynes, they were afraid that the operation of the system might lead to grave complications in the system of international finance. They were afraid that if Germany should be ruined by the harsh terms of the Peace Treaty it would mean a permanent loss of trade with a nation of over sixty million people. They did not realise at that time — indeed they could hardly be expected to realise it — that a day would come when twenty years' profit on trade with Germany would be wiped out by losses inflicted upon the City by air raid on one single night.

It was only natural that bankers and economists should view with grave concern the Damocles sword which was hanging over Germany's head in the form of reparations claims far in excess of her capacity to pay by means of the then generally accepted methods. Their concern grew as and when the volume of German short-term and long-term credits abroad increased, for any breakdown was bound to produce grave repercussions in countries which lent Germany the money paid in reparations. International financiers and millions of investors all over the world acquired a substantial vested interest in Germany's welfare. Obviously this development was not envisaged by the French statesmen of Versailles who imagined that they could secure indirect control over

Germany by means of fixing reparations claims at an astronomical figure far in excess of Germany's capacity to pay. They did not realise that a situation would arise in which any attempt on their part to enforce their claim, or, failing that, to assume the rôle of the bailiff and occupy German territory, would lead to an international financial crisis. At the time of the occupation of the Ruhr this situation did not yet exist, for prior to 1923 no foreign credits or loans were granted to Germany. From 1924 onwards, however, the extent to which any drastic French intervention in Germany was liable to upset the delicate international financial apparatus increased until the climax in 1931. The authors of the Treaty of Versailles failed to realise that the system of reparations which was then originated and subsequently developed would in practice tend to secure Germany against French intervention. Had the French negotiators at the Paris peace conference but foreseen this, they would not have consented to relinquish the idea of direct control over Germany in order to satisfy President Wilson. They did not realise that they relinquished the substance for the sake of the shadow.

CHAPTER IV

DURING the years that followed the conclusion of peace German people were simply oozing in self-pity. Admittedly, during the early years at any rate, they had good reason to be sorry for themselves. The collapse of the old régime was followed by a period of civil war and utter chaos. The transition from war economy to peace economy was even more difficult than in the victorious countries. Above all, extreme inflation inflicted considerable hardships upon all classes. And yet, if we compare the fate of the defeated German nation in 1918 with that of the nations conquered by Germany from 1939 onwards, we cannot help being struck by the fact that the German people were let off very lightly indeed. Apart from the provinces west of the Rhine, they were spared the presence of conquering enemy troops.

After their defeat the German people were left very much to their own devices to work out their own salvation the best way they could. No domineering occupation army was imposed upon them. Moreover, with the exception of a small part of Eastern Prussia, the territory of the Reich was entirely spared material destruction. While the finances of the Reich deteriorated, its material wealth, represented by townships, industries and other means of production, means of transport, art treasures, etc., remained substantially untouched by the war. From this point

44

of view Germany was incomparably better off than France with her vast devastated regions, or Belgium, Rumania, Poland, and Yugoslavia, which countries suffered the destruction of the war and exploitation by German occupation armies. Germany was even better off than Great Britain, which to some extent at any rate suffered material losses through air raids, and to a much larger extent through the sinking of her merchant ships.

The immense suffering which the German people had to go through during the years that followed the armistice was not due to any considerable extent to the peace treaty, but to the inability of the German nation to consolidate its new régime. Having grown accustomed to blind obedience, the German people were incapable of applying at a moment's notice an efficient system of democratic government. Amidst the confusion of class war and civil war the Republican Government was unable to assume sufficient authority to consolidate its finances and develop an economic policy to tide over the country from war economy to peace economy.

Admittedly, the excessive burden of reparations played a part in increasing the new Government's difficulties, but not to the extent to which German propaganda claims it to have done. For instance, the collapse of the mark in 1923 is attributed by German propaganda to reparations and to the Ruhr occupation. While it is beyond doubt that the effect of the reparations payments and the temporary loss of one of the most important industrial districts contributed towards advanced inflation, it is equally true that in its final stages that inflation was largely a gesture of desperate protest against the Ruhr occupation. By plunging into extreme inflation Germany was cutting off her nose to spite her face. It is beyond doubt that Germany had largely herself to blame for her sufferings between 1918 and 1923. The fact that it was possible to stabilise the currency and consolidate to some extent the German economic system while the Ruhr was still under French occupation, and before the system of reparations was consolidated in the Dawes scheme, shows that the collapse of the mark was by no means the inevitable consequence of the Peace Treaty.

Nevertheless, it became fashionable during the early post-war period to pity poor Germany. While in France the hatred aroused by the German invasion (the third within a century) remained strong long after the cessation of the hostilities, British people were ready to forgive and to forget almost immediately after the Armistice. Even though Mr. Lloyd George secured many millions of votes on the strength of his electioneering slogan " Hang the Kaiser " and on his promise to exact untold milliards of reparations from Germany, before many months it was evident that neither he nor the British nation meant this seriously. Throughout the subsequent years Mr. Lloyd George and his successors concentrated their efforts upon restraining France from being too harsh on Germany.

This attitude appeared at that time to be in accordance with the traditional balance of power policy of Great Britain. If we look back upon the early 'twenties it may appear absurd that after the defeat of Germany she should have been regarded as the weaker party compared with France. At the time, however, many of us allowed ourselves to be unduly influenced by the surface phenomenon of internal political disorganisation and financial chaos.

We did not adequately realise that the Peace Treaty left Germany, a nation of some sixty-five millions, more united than ever, with her gigantic industrial organisation intact ; and that in possession of man-power and industrial organisation she was in a position to reconstruct sooner or later the vast quantities of arms which she was compelled to surrender or destroy after the Armistice. This should have been obvious all the time, but many of us attached an exaggerated importance to the evidence of Germany's temporary weakness. It would have been in accordance with the balance of power policy to continue to support France after victory, because in spite of the rather unpleasantly aggressive militarism she developed between 1919 and 1924, she was still the weaker party in the long run. This was in fact the attitude of the Foreign Office. On the other hand, the Treasury and the Bank of England allowed their attitude to be influenced by the surface evidence of Germany's financial weakness and economic difficulties. Whitehall and Threadneedle Street both imagined to serve the balance of power policy by assisting Germany in her financial recovery. Those who supported this attitude — and I must confess I was among them — were guilty of grossly underestimating Germany's recuperative power.

From 1924 onwards the financial authorities and the financial community of Great Britain plunged themselves wholeheartedly into an effort to assist Germany financially. Even before 1924 there was evidence that financial interests in other countries were anxious to help. Until 1923 Germany paid reparations largely with the aid of the sales of mark notes abroad. It should have been obvious to anyone with common sense that in prevailing circumstances the mark was doomed. Nevertheless, there were thousands and thousands of people in every country who were eager to buy mark notes in the hope that some day they might appreciate. Pro-German banking interests were busily engaged in satisfying this demand by importing mark notes by the shipload. A most disgraceful traffic developed during the advanced phases of German inflation. Mark notes of large denomination were sold at street corners by agents of the banks in question at sixpence apiece at a time when the exchange value of the amount involved was a fraction of a penny. There was thus an ample margin of profit for the pro-German importers and also for the intermediaries. The assistance given to Germany during that phase was by no means unprofitable.

After 1924 financial assistance to Germany assumed much more " respectable " forms. To begin with, the Bank of England itself took charge of the issue of the British *tranche* of the Dawes Loan. From that time onwards until the Wall Street slump international banking houses in London and other financial centres were engaged in reckless competition in the issue of loans for German States, municipalities, industrial undertakings, etc. At the same time banks in the various lending centres were engaged in cut-throat competition in the granting of short-term credits to Germany at interest rates which barely covered the clerical work involved, and did not allow anything for risk.

Germany's ability to borrow on such a gigantic scale a few years after her bankruptcy through the depreciation of the mark was largely due to the widespread belief in the inherent honesty of the German

people.   Beyond doubt during the pre-war decades of
peace and prosperity Germany had acquired a first-
class reputation for commercial integrity.   It was
widely believed that even though circumstances between 1914 and 1924 may have forced her to depart
from her high principles, those circumstances were
not likely to recur and that Germany could therefore
be trusted implicitly.   This faith in Germany's pro-
verbial honesty was, and to some extent still is, largely
responsible for the pro-German sentiments which
seemed to survive all the disappointments caused by
bitter experience since the advent of the Nazi régime.
On close examination, however, it becomes evident
that the basis of Germany's honesty in the past was
not ethical but purely practical.   Before the last war
German bankers and merchants were honest because
it paid them to be honest.   They wanted to build up
goodwill and it would have been short-sighted to spoil
their chances to do so for the sake of passing profits
derived from dishonest dealing.   The experience of
those who had dealings with German business firms is,
however, that they ceased to be honest the moment
this ceased to be advantageous to them.   Firms which
had dealings with Germany over a number of years
had the experience that while the series of transactions
continued they could trust the German firms implicitly.
They had to take great care, however, that at the end
of the last transaction they should have no outstanding claims against the Germans because otherwise the latter were certain to find excuses for failing
to settle the balance due.   Having terminated the
series of transactions there was no point in remaining
honest and it became profitable to secure the advantage of dishonesty.   This experience repeated itself

during the period between the two wars on a gigantic scale. Investors and bankers engaged in lending to Germany during the 'twenties had no means of foreseeing this, however. They lived in a fools' paradise, fully convinced that they were doing well for themselves and helping poor downtrodden Germany at the same time.

The result of this generous influx of foreign loans was the development of a remarkable degree of prosperity. It enabled Germany to reconstruct the capital destroyed by advanced inflation in 1923. She was able to recover her foreign markets largely by means of selling abroad on a long-term credit basis. While British firms were unable to offer long-term credits to their foreign customers, their German rivals were able to do so, thanks to the money they borrowed in London. Short-term credits raised in London and New York were re-lent for periods of years to Russia and other countries in which Germany wanted to secure an economic foothold. At the same time, with the aid of British and American loans the German industries became rationalised to a considerable degree. The old-fashioned plants of British firms were at a grave disadvantage because, thanks to loans obtained in London, German industrialists were able to instal the most up-to-date machinery. We saw in the last chapter that borrowing abroad enabled Germany to construct model dwellings and sundry municipal buildings providing for the German people comfort, recreation and even luxury undreamt-of among the corresponding classes of British people.

Indeed, after Germany succeeded in overcoming the Ruhr occupation and until the Wall Street slump began to produce its effects, Germany had very little ground for complaining. Not having to spend milliards on the upkeep of a standing army, she was able to concentrate on social welfare expenditure. Even though prosperity between 1925 and 1930 did not reach the degree of pre-1914 prosperity, it was more widely spread and the working classes had a bigger share in it. And there appeared to be no reason why Germany should not reach and surpass her pre-1914 prosperity. Throughout the five or six years that preceded the Wall Street slump Germany received every possible assistance to enable her to recover her pre-war strength. Apart from the assistance granted under the auspices of British and other official quarters, she received as much money as she wanted from private interests. Indeed there was no need even for her borrowers to take the initiative : the money was brought to her doorsteps. During the middle 'twenties the luxury hotels of Berlin and the other leading German cities were always crowded with representatives of American issuing houses offering loans to potential German borrowers and competing recklessly with each other in order to secure the business. Never before in the history of modern finance was it so easy for any country to run up a big international indebtedness.

While American banks took a leading part in this issuing activity, London banking firms were a good second. What is more, it became a practice to place privately in London large amounts of the German dollar loans issued in New York by American banking houses. Even during the period when owing to the weakness of sterling an unofficial embargo was placed on public issues, the authorities raised no objections to such private placings. The Bank of England would have been well in a position to stop them, since most of them were arranged by banking firms represented on its board of directors. Mr. Montagu Norman would only have had to say the word. But he did not do so.

Nor did the authorities raise a finger to stop London banks from granting Germany excessive short-term credits. Competition for such credits was quite as keen as for the issue of long-term loans, with the result that the commission for German acceptance credits was reduced to the negligible figure of one-eighth per cent for three months. Since the German bills accepted by a first-class London bank were placeable at the prevailing discount rate for fine bank bills (which was between one-half per cent and one per cent) German borrowers were able to raise credits in London at a very low cost. They did not fail to abuse their privileged position. The volume of genuine bills they could draw against acceptance credits was limited by the volume of self-liquidating international commercial transactions. Since, however, it had been the practice of German firms to quote long-term credits for exports, the amount of genuine short-term credits was comparatively moderate. Consequently they abused their London short-term credit facilities by drawing purely fictitious finance bills against them and using the funds thus obtained under false pretences for financing long-term credit transactions.

When a lie is so obviously a lie that it deceives no one it thereby ceases to be a lie. There was not a single banker in London who was in doubt about the real character of the bills sent in to them for acceptance by German bankers. For one thing, hardly any of these bills were accompanied by documents — much to the relief of the more speculative types of banking houses which would have found it difficult to cope with the clerical work involved in handling large volumes of documentary bills. Apart from this, very frequently the total amount of the batch of bills sent in for acceptance was exactly equivalent to the round figure fixed as the limit of the acceptance credit facilities granted to the German bank concerned. To keep up appearances the bills were issued in odd amounts, but by a queer coincidence which was bordering on the miraculous their total was a round figure and exactly the figure of the credit granted.

The Bank of England was fully aware of what was happening. In accordance with its traditions it ought to have emphatically warned the acceptance houses and banks against this unsound practice leading to a deterioration of the quality of the sterling acceptance. No such warning was uttered at any time, even though it was generally known that about 75 per cent of the German bills in London were fictitious finance bills with no commercial backing behind them. When during the late 'twenties I criticised this practice in a number of articles in the *Financial News* and urged the authorities to discourage it, my protest was a lone voice crying in the wilderness. I made myself thoroughly unpopular (not for the first time nor for the last time) in banking circles, but before many years I had the melancholy satisfaction of having been vindicated by events. It was because of the lack of discrimination on the part of the banks in accepting German bills irrespective of whether they represented genuine trade transactions, and because of the Bank of England's unwillingness to discourage the practice and thereby to cause inconvenience to Germany, that the London banking community was caught in 1931

E

with unsecured credits amounting to over £40 million.

Mr. Norman's passive attitude towards the unsound German short-term financing in London was by no means the only indication of his pro-German policy. His attitude towards financial reconstruction on the Continent by means of officially negotiated loans, mostly under the auspices of the League of Nations, was also characterised by a rather one-sided tendency to assist Germany and her former allies. The countries which benefited by Mr. Norman's zeal for financial reconstruction were Austria, Hungary, Bulgaria, the Free City of Danzig, Greece and Estonia. The first three were Germany's comrades in arms during the last war. Danzig was essentially a German city. In the case of the Estonian loan the Bank of England made considerable efforts to induce the borrowing Government to arrange the issue through the Baltic German banking firm of Scheel & Co. It is true that the list includes Greece and does not include Turkey. Perhaps it is a mere coincidence that while Greece, though an ally of this country during the last war, restored the pro-German régime of King Constantine after the war, and Turkey, though an ally of Germany during the last war, adopted after the war a régime not friendly towards her former ally. Apart from Greece none of this country's former allies benefited by Mr. Norman's zeal for financial reconstruction. Yugoslavia, Rumania and Poland knocked at his door in vain. France had to work out her own salvation without any assistance whatever on the part of the Bank of England. Indeed, during the critical period in 1926 when it appeared as if the franc would follow the mark in its downward course, Mr. Norman purposely avoided breaking his journey in Paris on his way to the French Riviera, for, as he told a personal friend of his, he did not want to meet M. Poincaré in case he should ask him for something which he would have to refuse. With the sole exception of Belgium, which country was assisted to put the finishing touches to her financial reconstruction, the unwritten rule was that " Germany's former opponents need not apply". Yet the victors were as much in need of assistance in financial reconstruction as the vanquished nations.

Evidently Germany was being thoroughly pampered and spoiled. Notwithstanding this, she was still very far from being satisfied even during that period. The denunciation of the Treaty of Versailles remained the most popular slogan in politics. Even though Hitler's progress during that period was comparatively slow, other nationalist movements were gathering strength owing to the widespread resentment over the much-exaggerated grievances of the Versailles Treaty. The election of Field-Marshal Hindenburg to succeed as President the Socialist Ebert showed which way the wind blew. If the object of financial assistance to Germany was to appease her, its failure to achieve this aim was becoming increasingly evident.

Thanks to the loans and credits granted abroad, the Dawes scheme was working smoothly. The foreign exchange obtained from these loans enabled Germany to make the necessary transfers of payments in foreign currency. Nevertheless, it was becoming more and more obvious that Germany was making no payments in the genuine sense of the term, as she had no export surplus to enable her to do so. Needless to say, the main reason for this was that the foreign loans had enabled her to import too much. The only way in which a substantial export surplus could have been created was by means of a reduction of the standard of living of the German people. In fact there had been no such reduction. On the contrary, during the late 'twenties the Germans had nearly as high a standard of living as before the last war. The difference was that while before 1914 Germany was able to accumulate investments abroad in spite of her high standard of living, fifteen years later she was increasing her standard of living with the aid of borrowed money.

However it may be, it was evident that the high figure of reparations annuities made it futile even to attempt to cover the requirements by means of an export surplus. It was decided therefore to revise the Dawes scheme and to operate a scheme which would reduce the annuities and which would at the same time enable the recipients of reparations to commercialise at least part of their claims. Accordingly the Young Committee was set up in 1929 and worked out a new reparations plan which was subsequently embodied in the Hague agreement of 1930.

While the amount of the annuities was not reduced very drastically, a new apparatus was set up for the purpose of securing the smooth transfer of reparations. This apparatus was the Bank for International Settlements. Germany was given a permanent place in the organisation of this bank. She was represented on its Board by three Directors against Great Britain's two representatives. It was only with difficulty that Germany was persuaded to relinquish her claim that the post of General Manager should be filled by a German. The two British representatives were Mr. Montagu Norman and Sir Otto Niemeyer. During the course of the heated controversies of the

years that followed the establishment of the Bank for
International Settlements there were frequent clashes
at the Board meetings at Basle between the German
and French Directors. In the majority of known
instances the British Directors gave their support to
their German colleagues, We shall see in a later
chapter the part played by the Bank for International
Settlements after the German occupation of Czecho-
Slovakia. At this stage it is sufficient to point out
that the activities of that bank provided Mr. Norman
with fresh opportunities for making himself felt in a
sense favourable to the appeasement of Germany.

CHAPTER V

THE CRISIS OF 1931

BEYOND doubt ten years after the conclusion of the Treaty of Versailles Germany achieved a high degree of prosperity. If the Treaty of Versailles had been as wicked and cruel as German propaganda, supported by the "*mea culpa*" school in Great Britain and elsewhere, claims it to be, Germany could not possibly have achieved such a degree of prosperity. She would have been bled white by ruthless exploitation under the régime imposed upon her by the Peace Treaty. Her standard of living would have declined to sub-sistence level. Her social welfare institutions would have deteriorated, for a country so ruthlessly exploited as Germany was supposed to be under the Treaty of Versailles could really ill-afford to improve or even maintain the living conditions of its working classes. What are the facts? Impartial economists were almost unanimous in agreeing that after 1924 Germany underwent a spectacular recovery in every sense. On the basis of official German facts and figures it was impossible to avoid reaching this conclusion, which in any case was amply confirmed by the impressions of foreign observers travelling in Germany. From the point of view of economic conditions ten years after the end of the war Germany had indeed no ground for complaint. Admittedly, she improved her stand-ard of living, her social institutions and her capital investments largely on borrowed money. But then

that was her creditors' concern. If foreign financiers
and investors chose to sink milliards into Germany
at a time when the huge political liability of reparations was still hanging over her head, it was not for
the German people to complain.

From a political point of view there was hardly
more justification for dissatisfaction. It is true some
of the disabilities imposed upon Germany by the
Treaty of Versailles were still in force ten years after
its conclusion. The most important among these
disabilities was that Germany was not allowed to
rearm. It is difficult to see, however, why this fact
should have affected the welfare of the German people.
Nobody threatened Germany with invasion during the
period that followed the evacuation of the Ruhr.
Even though for all practical purposes she was defenceless, no country sought to take advantage of it. What
is more, in spite of her disarmed state Germany was
able to make herself felt in the councils of nations to
an increasing degree. The Rhineland was evacuated
by the Allies long before the period for its occupation
fixed by the Peace Treaty expired. Germany was
admitted to the League of Nations and was given a
permanent seat on its Council. At the meetings at
Geneva her voice carried considerable weight.

It is true the colonies which she lost as a result
of the last war remained under British, French or
Japanese mandates. The Mandatory Powers, however, adopted the policy of the open door, and German
pre-war colonists returned to their former residences
in great numbers. In the case of some of the colonies
under British mandate, trade with Germany reached
its pre-1914 level. In any case, even in the absence
of colonies, Germany was able to expand considerably

her foreign trade and to compete successfully with her British trade rivals, not only in foreign markets, but to a large extent even in the British Empire and in Great Britain itself. Her " living space " was the whole world. She was able to buy and sell on the five continents, and there was no need for her either to possess political control over her markets and raw-material resources or to possess a huge army and navy to increase her weight for the purposes of her commercial negotiations.

Evidently, from the point of view of Germany's prosperity, the disabilities imposed upon her by the Treaty of Versailles were of no importance. The sole reasons why she resented these disabilities were considerations of vanity and prestige. Yet Germany under the Weimar Republic enjoyed considerable prestige during the late 'twenties, in spite of the fact that she had no army or colonies, owing to her remarkable achievements in the sphere of literature, science, arts, etc. German literature in particular assumed easily a leading position in Europe during the 'twenties. The whole world was duly impressed by Germany's cultural achievements during that period. That is, the whole world with the exception of Germany herself. Her deeply ingrained spirit of militarism could not be eradicated in the lifetime of one generation. To the German mind prestige remained equivalent to military power — the ability to achieve diplomatic victories with the aid of sabre-rattling, and to bully and overawe other nations. The German nation was entirely unable to appreciate the prestige it enjoyed abroad for its peaceful achievements. It was even unable to enjoy its diplomatic successes, such as the premature evacuation of the

Rhineland, since these successes were achieved by peaceful negotiations instead of through the weight of its armed strength. In one word the German people was determined to be unhappy about Versailles and to consider itself to be aggrieved and downtrodden.

Before very long after the tenth anniversary of the Treaty of Versailles there was a turn in world trend which brought about a fundamental change in the situation in Germany. Following upon the Wall Street slump of November 1929, a world-wide economic depression developed culminating in the financial crises of 1931 to 1933. Although, as I pointed out in Chapter III, the reparations clauses of the Treaty of Versailles contributed towards increasing the vulnerability of the international financial system, the fundamental causes of the depression were quite independent of the terms of the Peace Treaty.

The first great slump that followed the war of 1914–1918 was also of considerable violence and of long duration, because the war unsettled the international economic system and increased the vulnerability of the financial superstructure. Between the slump of 1920 and that of 1930 the vulnerability of the financial superstructure increased further as a result of over-trading, over-speculation, the mismanagement of monetary policies and many other reasons unconnected with the terms of the Peace Treaty. Above all, the inadequacy of the old-fashioned system of *laissez-faire* had to produce its effect. Even under the comparatively stable conditions prevailing before the last war the absence of economic planning carried its penalty from time to time in the form of periodically recurrent economic crises. The dimensions of these crises were bound to increase, partly as a result of the spectacular increase in the volume of fictitious wealth that accumulated through the war, in consequence of which the figures involved grew to a multiple of those involved in previous crises.

Another development which bore a large share in the responsibility for the gravity of the crisis during the 'thirties was the progress in the rationalisation of industrial and agricultural production. Now, under a planned society such progress would have worked out for the benefit of mankind. Under *laissez-faire*, however, it resulted in huge unsaleable surpluses of wheat and other agricultural products leading to a slump affecting the greater half of mankind engaged in agricultural production. Rationalisation in industries resulted in unemployment, which became aggravated as a result of the agricultural depression. The next phase in the vicious circle was that the purchasing power of the industrial population became reduced and demand for land products further declined, and so on and so forth.

It would be possible to continue to give many more reasons which to a larger or less degree contributed towards the economic difficulties of the 'thirties. The above casual observations should be sufficient, however, to show that the main factors were much more fundamental than the terms of the Treaty of Versailles. In all probability the crisis would have arisen even in the absence of unreasonable terms regarding reparations. And there is not the slightest reason to doubt that Germany would have had her own share in the world-wide depression even if there had been no such thing as the Treaty of Versailles and even if no reparations payments had ever been imposed upon her. After all, the United States did not lose the war, nor did she have to pay reparations, and in spite of that she was affected by the crisis at least to the same extent as Germany.

Owing to the unpopularity of the Treaty of Versailles in Germany, however, it was very easy for Hitler and other demagogues to make political capital out of Germany's share in the world-wide depression and to attribute her sufferings to the Treaty of Versailles. Since that treaty was hated by the millions of the German people they readily absorbed the entirely unfounded assertions that their sufferings through the world economic crisis were due to the wicked Allied statesmen of Versailles. It is this exploitation of the crisis for political propaganda and not the terms of the treaty itself that assisted Hitler in increasing the number of his supporters in the 'thirties.

The climax was reached in 1931 when the failure of the Austrian Creditanstalt provided a signal for a sweeping flight of short-term capital from Germany and Central Europe. The difficulties of the Creditanstalt were not due to the Treaty of Versailles. Judging by the extent to which the bank recovered during the last few years of Austria's independence it is now almost generally admitted that its position in 1931 was inherently sound. Had it not been for the international political tension caused by an attempt to establish a Customs union between Germany and Austria the bank would in all probability have overcome its temporary difficulties.

The collapse of the Creditanstalt gave rise to a panic which led to a moratorium in Germany and to the suspension of the gold standard in Great Britain.

In the eleventh hour efforts were made to avert the disaster. On the initiative of President Hoover the payment of reparations and inter-Allied debts was suspended for twelve months. Even before that the British authorities made an effort to salvage the Creditanstalt. That these efforts failed to produce the desired effect was largely the result of the narrow and short-sighted policy pursued by M. Laval, who was then French Prime Minister. Since in the meantime he has become the leading exponent of the policy of French co-operation with Germany against Great Britain, it is perhaps worth while to recall that in 1931 it was his unreasoning nationalism and obstinacy that prevented the Anglo-American attempt at salvage from producing its results.

It is perhaps also worth while to recall that the uncompromising attitude adopted by M. Laval was largely due to the attitude of the so-called moderate Government of Dr. Brüning which insisted upon a Customs union between Germany and Austria. This fact goes a long way towards proving that even under the Weimar régime Germany's foreign policy was fundamentally expansionist, and that the seeds of the Austrian *Anschluss* of 1938 were sown by democratic German statesmen such as Stresemann and Brüning.

Admittedly, had it not been for the reparations Germany's short-term indebtedness in 1931 would have been incomparably smaller and the international panic would have affected her banking system to a much less extent. Even in the absence of a banking crisis, however, Germany would have suffered through the repercussions of the international financial crisis. Her export trade would have contracted and her unemployment would have increased, even though not to the same extent as it actually did.

However this may be, by 1931 Germany had
genuine reason to be sorry for herself. Apart from
the general considerations indicated above, there were
specific reasons why the crisis should be one of
exceptional gravity in Germany. As I pointed out
earlier, thanks to the loans obtained from foreign
countries Germany rationalised her industries to a
very large degree, and thereby a large number of
workmen were thrown out of employment. Had
rationalisation been carried out gradually this would
have been avoided. As it was the crisis came before
the hands released through rationalisation could be
reabsorbed.

What is perhaps an even more important consideration, wholesale unemployment was quite unnecessarily
exaggerated from 1931 onwards by the ultra-orthodox
monetary policy pursued by Dr. Brüning's Government. The obvious step in face of the flight from the
mark would have been a devaluation, especially after
the depreciation of sterling in the autumn of 1931
had placed German trade at a grave disadvantage in
face of British competition. The German Government
refused, however, to consider this obvious step. To
avoid it a deflationary policy was embarked upon, and
credit restrictions brought about a contraction in
industrial production in addition to the fall caused by
the loss of foreign markets through the overvaluation
of the reichsmark. All this could have been avoided
if Germany had devalued her currency or if she had
joined the sterling bloc. It is true a devaluation or
depreciation of the reichsmark would have increased
the reichsmark equivalent of German foreign debts.
Since, however, the payment of these debts was in

any case suspended, this would not have mattered very much. In fact as a result of the devaluation the exchange position of the Reich would have improved, and she would have been able to relax her restrictions on the transfer of payments on account of foreign debts. It is possible that had Dr. Brüning followed a sensible monetary policy in 1931–1932 an improvement in the trade position would have weakened the popular support to Hitler.

While Germany suffered considerably through the world-wide crisis, at the same time she also derived considerable benefit by it, since it led to the cancellation of reparations. The first stage towards this was the Hoover Moratorium of 1931. This was followed twelve months later by the Lausanne Conference at which it was agreed to reduce the total of reparations to a fraction of their original amount. None of the participants at the Lausanne Conference had the agreement ratified, so that it became a dead letter and no claim was ever made against Germany for even the moderate amounts fixed at Lausanne. Reparations simply faded out. The explanation of the willingness of France to make this sweeping concession to Germany was that the international financial crisis resulted in a sharp conflict between British and French opinion. British official circles, especially the Treasury and the Bank of England, held the view that the unsatisfactory state of the reparations problem was largely responsible for the crisis and that its settlement would go a long way towards preparing the way for recovery. This view was shared by a very large section of British opinion, which was becoming increasingly anti-French owing to M. Laval's stubborn resistance to any reasonable revision of

reparations. France was widely regarded as the main
obstacle to financial stabilisation and economic recovery. This view was widely adopted also in other
countries, so that France found herself isolated. At
the election of April 1932, M. Laval suffered a decisive
defeat and was succeeded by M. Herriot, who adopted
a more conciliatory attitude.

At the same time, the evidence that France was
now inclined to pursue a policy of moderation encouraged the revival of aggressive nationalism in
Germany. It is perhaps more than coincidence that
a few weeks after the French election results President
Hindenburg should dismiss Dr. Brüning and replace
him by von Papen.

After this change reparations were obviously dead.
All that remained to be done was to bury them.
This was accomplished at Lausanne in such a way
as to save the face of all parties. There was indeed
no alternative for France but to acquiesce. Any
attempt to insist on reparations and to collect them
if necessary by means of an occupation of the Ruhr
would have aggravated further the international
financial crisis and the world-wide depression, and
would therefore have aroused very strong anti-French
feelings. Needless to say, France would have been
quite able to deal with Germany single-handed, but
throughout the post-war period all French Governments holding office were extremely anxious to avoid
her becoming isolated. Thus it was that the biggest
concession since the conclusion of the Peace Treaty
was granted to Germany a few weeks after the advent
of the openly nationalistic von Papen Government.

Owing to the development of the international
political and financial situation during the spring of

1932, it was considered safe in Germany to become openly nationalistic. Until then the Governments of Stresemann and Brüning kept up a pretence of complying with the terms of the Peace Treaty while making slow preparations to enable Germany to scrap it. These preparations became considerably accentuated after the advent of the von Papen Government. Since France relaxed her grip, Germany could afford to become openly aggressive. The major act of appeasement of the Lausanne Agreement stimulated her aggressive spirit — an experience which was to repeat itself many times during the subsequent years.

CHAPTER VI

IT is repeated to boredom by the "*mea culpa*" school
that the advent of Hitler had been the natural, logical
and inevitable sequence of the Treaty of Versailles.
Beyond doubt the extreme exaggeration of Germany's
grievances arising from that treaty assisted Hitler to
no slight extent to increase his popularity. At the
same time, however, he would not have been given
an opportunity to seize power had it not been for
the monetary situation in Germany in 1923 and again
in 1933. Hitler's Party was born in inflation ; it rose
to power in deflation. Even in the absence of these
factors and of any genuine grievances through the
Peace Treaty, the Junker landowners and their allies,
the wealthy industrialists, would have gradually
wrested the power from the Weimar régime. As it
was they tried to make use of the popularity of
Hitler's movement, only to find that they got more
than they had been bargaining for.

Hitler was brought to power by Junkers and
industrialists. His advent was welcomed consequently
among their opposite numbers in Great Britain, who
hailed him as the saviour of Germany from Communism. Needless to say, apart from the chaotic
years that followed the Armistice there was never any
real chance for Communism in Germany to secure a
majority in Parliament, nor to overthrow the Republican régime by unconstitutional means. By 1933 the

German Communists became an almost respectable Parliamentary Party with a considerable nuisance value but without any possibility of assuming control. Nor was world revolution in general and revolution in Germany in particular very actively fostered from Moscow by 1933. By that time Soviet Russia had joined the League of Nations and settled down to peaceful collaboration with the other Powers. Litvinoff believed in a conciliatory foreign policy, while Stalin was too much interested in his Five-Year Plan and other internal matters to pay much attention to foreign affairs.

Nevertheless Nazi propaganda, representing Hitler as a modern St. George slaying the Bolshevik dragon, went down very well in British reactionary circles. So much so that they prepared to ignore his openly declared policy aiming at scrapping the Treaty of Versailles and conquering the European continent. It was widely felt in British political and financial circles that such a useful bulwark against Communism as Hitler deserved sympathy and support.

Moreover, in spite of the advent of a strongly nationalistic régime in Germany it was still widely believed in influential quarters in London that she was the weaker party and as such was entitled to British support, in accordance with the traditional balance of power policy. The excesses committed by the Nazis from the very first moment they assumed power were generously overlooked, on the ground that "the poor Germans had suffered so much under the cruel Treaty of Versailles that they could hardly be blamed for being thoroughly bad-tempered and intolerant". It was widely believed that these excesses would gradually subside as and when Germany's position improved and her grievances were remedied.

Even the default on Germany's external debts by the Nazi Government failed at first to arouse antagonism. Evidently the reason for the default was that in an effort to reduce unemployment Hitler began to spend milliards on public works and rearmament, and this inevitably reacted upon Germany's exports and imports. The apologists of the Nazi régime pointed out that, after all, the solution of the problem of wholesale unemployment had to be Hitler's primary consideration. But then, this problem could have been remedied to a very large extent through the devaluation of the reichsmark, which would have improved the German trade balance, while the policy chosen by Hitler caused it to deteriorate. Moreover, a large and increasing proportion of German abnormal expenditure was for the purposes of warlike preparation. Even when this became evident it failed to alter the attitude of pro-German financial and political circles.

In May 1933 Germany's foreign creditors were surprised one day to receive a cable from Berlin announcing that all external debt payments were suspended and that they were expected in Berlin at a given date to negotiate with the Reichsbank. The manner in which this default was brought about caused considerable indignation. It was somewhat unusual for creditors to be ordered by their defaulting debtor in a barrack-square style to present themselves before the debtor at a fixed hour. Unfortunately this shock failed to result in the necessary unity between the various groups of creditors. Hitler's financial wizard, Dr. Schacht, succeeded in playing them off against each other and thereby preventing the establishment of a united front. When on May 29, 1933, the representatives of the short-term banking creditors arrived in Berlin, their chief object was to secure from Dr. Schacht preferential treatment to the detriment of the long-term creditors. Realising that the amount Dr. Schacht was prepared to devote to the service of external debt was limited, they did their best to ensure that the bulk of that amount should be reserved for them rather than for their clients who had bought the long-term loans on their recommendation. Dr. Schacht was perfectly willing to satisfy them in this respect. A confidential report submitted to the Committee of Banking Creditors by one of the British delegates, the Hon. R. H. Brand, states that in order to ascertain Dr. Schacht's attitude on this matter a lunch was arranged between him and the other British banking delegate, Mr. F. C. Tiarks, who found Dr. Schacht's attitude wholly satisfactory from the point of view of the short-term creditors. Mr. Brand remarked in his report that throughout the negotiations Dr. Schacht treated them with courtesy and addressed the bankers as " colleagues " — though why it should be considered a high honour to be addressed as " colleague " by a defaulting debtor is not obvious at first sight.

This concrete instance is characteristic of the lack of unity between various groups of Germany's creditors. Had it been possible to establish a united front, conceivably it would have been possible to induce the authorities to take a firm line in dealing with Germany. As a matter of fact, in June 1934 the Treasury felt impelled to take a firm line, because of Germany's threatened default upon current commercial liabilities. This would have meant a blow to

Lancashire and other industrial areas, and the Government could ill-afford to antagonise a large and influential section of the electorate by failing to safeguard its interests and by allowing unemployment to increase through the difficulties caused by the default. Accordingly, arrangements were made to collect the claims by means of compulsory exchange clearing. The Debts Clearing Offices Act was rushed through in Parliament unopposed. The moment Germany realised that the Government meant business, arrangements were made to resume payment of current commercial debts owed to British exporters. It might have been possible to carry the pressure further and insist upon a more favourable treatment of other classes of British creditors of Germany. Indeed, a former German high official who took an active part in the negotiations told me some years later that they could never understand why the British negotiators failed to insist upon more favourable terms. Germany was allowed to pocket year after year the proceeds of large export surpluses in her trade with Great Britain, and at the same time she reduced the service of her debt owed to British creditors to a fraction of the amounts due under the contracts.

Certain banking circles were at that time not anxious to squeeze Germany for larger payments even for their own benefit, let alone for the benefit of long-term creditors. A very large section of the British financial Press never missed an opportunity of putting in a word in excuse of the German attitude. The apologists of Germany's default were at pains to explain that they strongly disapproved of the Nazi excesses and that they were not even pro-German but simply pro-Schacht. They were anxious that Dr. Schacht's moderating influence should not be weakened by any uncompromising attitude on the part of the British Government or British financial interests. I pointed out at the time that it was most unlikely that Hitler should allow himself to be influenced by Dr. Schacht or anyone else once he considers the time ripe for resorting to aggressive action. Indeed, as we shall see later, at the beginning of 1938 Dr. Schacht was discarded after having lost his influence some two years earlier. There is no reason to suppose that in the absence of appeasement for the special benefit of Dr. Schacht Hitler would have invaded Austria, Czecho-Slovakia or Poland earlier than he actually did. He embarked upon these adventures when German rearmament reached a sufficiently advanced stage. Had Germany been compelled to relinquish some foreign exchange in favour of her foreign creditors as a result of strong pressure, there would have been less foreign exchange available for raw materials for rearmament purposes. Consequently it is possible that Hitler's aggressive moves might have been delayed.

The experience of June 1934, when the passing of the Debts Clearing Offices Act induced the German Government to improve its offer to British commercial creditors, shows that it would have been possible to secure advantages for British interests by means of a firmer policy. There was indeed every reason for Germany to make sacrifices in order to avoid exchange clearing with Great Britain. Year after year she had a considerable export surplus on her British trade, and it was the sterling thus obtained which largely financed her imports for the purposes of rearmament. Part of the sterling proceeds of German exports might easily have been seized for the benefit of British creditors. In spite of this, it was only with the utmost reluctance that the British authorities took advantage of Germany's fears of an exchange clearing. The Bank of England was strongly opposed to the exchange clearing system even at a time when it was employed successfully by a large and increasing number of countries. Banking interests in general were afraid that the exchange clearing system might deprive them of part of their banking business. For this reason there was general relief in the City when in June 1934 a Payments Agreement was concluded with Germany providing for the settlement of the commercial arrears and obviating the necessity for imposing exchange clearing on her.

This Payments Agreement worked most unsatisfactorily and by the autumn of 1934 it was on the verge of a breakdown. At this moment, however, the Bank of England stepped in and granted a credit to the Reichsbank in order to tide over the difficulties. Had it not been for this credit the failure of the Payments Agreement would have had to be openly admitted and it would have become necessary to resort to exchange clearing. As it was, the Payments Agreement was patched up. Germany continued to collect the free sterling proceeds of her export surplus and continued to grant most unsatisfactory terms to her British creditors.

It would have been very easy at that stage to strangle financially the Nazi régime and to compel Germany to revert to a more moderate foreign policy. For Germany depended to a very large extent upon the goodwill of Great Britain for her foreign trade. Apart altogether from her substantial export surplus to Great Britain — about which more will be said in Chapter VIII — she was enabled to have a series of favourable trade balances with most countries in Northern and Western Europe, thanks to Great Britain's willingness to accept an unfavourable trade balance in her relations with these countries. Sweden, for example, had a large export surplus in relation to Great Britain and spent a large part of the proceeds in Germany. By adopting the policy of bilateralism in foreign trade, which I strongly advocated at that time, it would have been possible to compel all these countries to spend on British goods the proceeds of their exports to Great Britain. As a result, German exports would have contracted sharply. This would have compelled Germany to abandon her ambitious rearmament drive and to pursue a moderate foreign policy. It might even have brought about a financial crisis of first-rate magnitude which would have driven the Nazis out of office. While it would have been perhaps too much to expect the Government to resort to such a Machiavellian policy, the Bank of England's action in coming to the rescue of the Reichsbank and of the Hitler régime was certainly uncalled for.

This was by no means the only manifestation of the Bank of England's favourable attitude towards Germany. Throughout the early years of the Nazi régime it abstained from bringing pressure to bear upon Germany's London banking creditors to induce them to cut their losses and liquidate at least part of their commitments. From the very outset American, French, Dutch and Swiss banking creditors were liquidating their German credits as fast as they could. The extent to which this was done by British banking creditors was, however, negligible. The banks themselves are largely to blame for the implicit faith they had in Germany. While they may not have been in a position to foresee future developments, it must have been obvious to official quarters that Hitler's aggressive policy carried to its logical conclusion was bound to lead to war eventually. It would have been, therefore, the duty of the Treasury and of the Bank of England to warn bankers and induce them to liquidate part of their frozen German credits. This was not done, however, and the authorities are therefore largely to blame for the fact that while other foreign banking creditors reduced their German commitments to a moderate amount, the City was caught with some £36 million at the outbreak of the war. This was a small part of the price this country had to pay for its policy of appeasement.

To have omitted to liquidate old credits was bad enough ; to have granted new credits was much worse. Yet this was actually done by a number of London banks during 1936 and 1937, even though the aggressive nature of Hitler's foreign policy was becoming increasingly obvious. Admittedly, the amounts involved were moderate in comparison with the total of outstanding German liabilities. Nevertheless, there was no justification for granting new credit facilities to a defaulting debtor. Apart altogether from political considerations, these transactions were unsound on purely financial grounds. By that time German rearmament was in full swing and Goering's Air Force was growing at an alarming pace. Notwithstanding this, credits were granted for the purpose of facilitating the import of raw materials by Germany for rearmament requirements. Conceivably, in the majority of instances the credits were not used directly for that purpose. Nevertheless, this made no difference on balance, since other resources which would otherwise have had to be used for essential civilian requirements became released for rearmament requirements, thanks to the new credits granted by the London banks. Moreover, there were actually instances in which German firms engaged in rearmament succeeded in obtaining new credits in London. For instance, the I. G. Farbenindustrie, probably the largest manufacturer of poison gas in the world, received new credits from at least two London banking houses.

Towards the end of 1936 a new firm was registered in London under the name of Compensation Brokers, Ltd., which was controlled by the banking houses of J. H. Schroeder & Co., and Hambros Bank, Ltd., and by the metal broker firm of C. Tennant Sons & Co., Ltd., with the declared object of assisting in financing barter transactions between Germany and various part sof the British Empire. The same firm is known to have made efforts to arrange and finance such barter transactions also between Germany and various European countries such as Spain, Rumania, Hungary, etc.

Neither the activities of this firm nor the granting of new credits by various London banks, which was generally known and could not escape the attention of the authorities, met with any official objections. Indeed, when the matter was repeatedly raised in Parliament, the Government spokesmen invariably refused to express any disapproval of such trans-actions. In one instance the then Financial Secretary to the Treasury, Mr. W. S. Morrison, went so far as to state actually that the Treasury had nothing against them. As a result of persistent criticism in Parliament and in the Press during the spring of 1937, however, the Bank of England sent out a circular to the banks at the Treasury's request, asking them to abstain as far as possible from granting any new credits to Germany. The practice of granting new credits was consequently discontinued. The fact that it was allowed to continue until outside pressure was brought to bear upon the authorities shows the strength of the current of appeasement that prevailed at the time.

It is only fair to make it clear that from the time of the Austrian *Anschluss*, when Germany's aggressive intentions became evident to all but the most gullible, the banking community in general changed its attitude in the matter of German credits. There was no longer any need for official pressure to induce most bankers to refrain from granting new credits. They were in fact anxious to recover some of their old credits under the Standstill Agreement. By that time, however, it was not very easy to liquidate German credits, even at the cost of cutting substantial losses. Most London bankers missed their chance during earlier years.

The only way through which it might still have been possible to reduce pre-1931 banking credits to Germany would have been through the establishment of exchange clearing. The question arose in connection with the German default upon Austria's foreign liabilities. While Austria's gold and foreign assets held in Great Britain were cheerfully surrendered to Germany after the *Anschluss*, this did not prevent the German Government from attempting to repudiate the Austrian external loans. The display of such a

degree of impudence made even the worms of appeasement turn. Negotiations conducted in Berlin by
Sir Frederick Leith-Ross were broken off and the
Government made it plain that this time it was
determined to apply exchange clearing. It went
even further and resorted to an amusing ruse quite
unusual in British diplomatic practice. It had forms
printed for the requirements of the Anglo-German
clearing and the British Commercial Counsellor in
Berlin had these forms conspicuously displayed on
his desk when receiving the visit of a German official.
During their conversation he was called away and
left the room for a sufficiently long time to give his
visitor a chance to study the literature so carelessly
exhibited. Within a few hours the German Government announced that it was prepared to reconsider
its attitude regarding the Austrian external loans.
The negotiations were resumed in London. They
were not proceeding very smoothly, however, and on
at least one occasion there was a possibility of a
breakdown. Thereupon an official paid a visit to the
German delegation and sent in his card specially
printed for that purpose, on which he described himself as Controller of the Anglo-German Clearing. He
explained to the German negotiators that since he
was going to be in charge of the clearing between the
two countries he wished to make personal contact
with his prospective German opposite number. His
reception was polite but not exactly cordial, but after
this there was no difficulty in coming to terms with
the Germans regarding the Austrian external loans.

During this tension the Association of British
Chambers of Commerce issued a statement declaring
itself emphatically in favour of the adoption of

exchange clearing. No such statement was forth-
coming from the representative organisation of British
bankers. Evidently the bankers were still prepared
to forego their chances of obtaining the repayment of
part of their standstill credits, rather than declare
themselves in favour of exchange clearing. Yet the
experience of June 1938 made it quite obvious that
the mere threat of exchange clearing was amply
sufficient to induce Germany to make concessions.
The reason why that threat could not be applied even
more effectively was that the German authorities
were fully aware of the unpopularity of the idea of
exchange clearing in Threadneedle Street and in
British banking circles in general. They knew they
could rely upon the British bankers to fight their
battle in this sphere.

Later, when it became obvious that war was a
mere question of time, most bankers would have been
willing to put up even with exchange clearing in
order to collect some of their claims. It was impossible,
however, to induce the Treasury to take a firm line.
By that time political appeasement was reigning
supreme and the last thing the Government wanted
to do was to irritate Germany by pressing her for
debt repayment.

In the absence of adequate official support the
bankers had but little chance to obtain any concessions from Germany. Throughout the annual
negotiations for the renewal of the Standstill Agreement the representatives of the Reichsbank and of
the German debtors adopted a thoroughly uncompromising attitude towards the representatives of
British banking creditors. The task of the latter was
anything but easy, since they were not adequately

backed up by the Treasury or even by the Bank of
England even at a time when Mr. Norman's word
carried weight with Dr. Schacht.   Nevertheless it
seems that the British negotiators did not take full
advantage of such limited chances as they had.   The
London bankers hoped that Mr. Tiarks, through his
excellent connections with influential German quarters,
might be able to secure for them some advantages.
This was not, however, the case, and Mr. Tiarks
became subject to much criticism in banking circles
by 1938–1939.   Discontent with his attitude rose to
a climax after he made a statement at the Cologne
Chamber of Commerce in March 1939, declaring that
British banks should not endeavour to reduce their
standstill credits to Germany.   His fellow-delegate,
Mr. R. H. Brand, was all too conciliatory, as we
saw earlier in this chapter.   Even though later his
attitude towards Germany changed, he failed to make
himself felt.   The third negotiator, Mr. Lidbury,
of the Westminster Bank, who was subsequently
included in the delegation to stiffen their attitude,
was doing his best, but was unable to achieve much
in the unequal contest.

A volume could be written on the ingenious ways
in which Germany managed to bamboozle her British
banking creditors.   Possibly one day I may undertake
the task, in which case the title of the book will be
" Standstill Credits : A Study in Gullibilities ".   To
give only one characteristic example : In 1937 the
standstill negotiators triumphantly announced to the
world that they succeeded in obtaining an important
concession from the German debtors.   Henceforth
a licence fee would be charged on the sales of travel
marks and the proceeds of this licence fee would be

distributed among the standstill creditors. It took some time for the creditors to realise that in practice they were being paid with their own money.

After Dr. Schacht's dismissal in January 1938, it became obvious that the policy of appeasing Germany by means of financial concessions for the sake of consolidating Dr. Schacht's position had failed. This fact opened the eyes of a number of bankers and, generally speaking, it is true that from that time the centre of gravity of the appeasement movement shifted westwards from the banking district of the City. Nevertheless, as we shall see in later chapters, appeasement in certain parts of the City survived Dr. Schacht.

CHAPTER VII

GUNS *AND* BUTTER FOR GERMANY

AT a comparatively early phase of German rearmament Goering declared that the German people prefer guns to butter. This ominous declaration should in itself have been sufficient to make Germany's aggressive intentions plain and to discourage appeasement. Nevertheless, the appeasement school made a valiant effort to out-Goering Goering and to improve upon his formula. Their declared aim was that Germany should be able to obtain guns *and* butter.

As a matter of fact, it would have been a mistake to take Goering too literally. The last thing he had in mind was to renounce butter for the sake of guns. (Judging by the obvious increase in his own avoirdupois during that period, he certainly did not sacrifice his butter ration for the sake of increasing the number of guns available for Germany.) It is true that the civilian population was made to do without many things for years in order to increase the resources available for raw materials for the requirements of rearmament. Germany's policy was, however, to aim at maintaining her civilian imports as far as possible, in spite of the gigantic abnormal import requirements brought about by the unprecedented arms drive. To rearm within a few years to the extent Germany had done between 1933 and 1939 would have overtaxed the resources of any country. Germany considered it, however, to be within her inalienable rights

to secure all her abnormal rearmament requirements
in addition to her normal civilian requirements. And
since the latter could not be covered entirely because
of the priority of the former, Germany worked up a
grievance against the world in general and against
the alleged British policy of economic encirclement
in particular.

She was complaining bitterly that she was deprived
of her *Lebensraum*. She claimed it as a right that
she should be placed in a position in which her requirements are fully satisfied in spite of their abnormal
increase through record rearmament. In this connection *Lebensraum* may be defined as the territory
designed to supply Germany with normal rations of
butter, in addition to satisfying her abnormal requirements of guns.

An article appearing in *The Times* long after the
outbreak of the war, endorsed by editorial comment,
put forward the argument that one of the causes
of the war was Germany's inability to expand her
foreign trade sufficiently. The truth of the matter is
that had Germany been satisfied with a more or less
normal tempo in rearmament she would have found no
difficulty whatever in meeting all her normal foreign
trade requirements. It is because she was determined
to spend gigantic sums on rearmament that such
difficulties as she experienced during the years before
the war had arisen. But then, surely it is hardly
reasonable to blame the democratic countries for their
unwillingness to go out of their way to facilitate
Germany's task of rearming, when the purpose for
which she was rearming in such an abnormal haste
was only too evident. Yet this is exactly the line
followed by those in favour of economic appeasement.

G

They left no stone unturned to enable Germany to secure for herself all the guns and all the butter she required.

We saw in the last chapter that the Government was unwilling to take any action which might have resulted in a reduction in the free sterling Germany obtained over a series of years through her foreign trade to this country and to other countries. Obvious as it was that the proceeds of German exports were spent largely on rearmament, the appeasement school strongly opposed any suggestion aiming at the reduction of Germany's free sterling surplus. The view was held in appeasement circles that any attempt at " squeezing " Germany in that direction would lead her to the conclusion that she must secure her *Lebensraum* by means of armed force. In the light of subsequent events it is now obvious to everybody that Germany meant to have her war in any case. The result of appeasement in this sphere was simply to enable her to import the necessary raw materials within a shorter time than she would otherwise have been able to.

There was no need whatever for this country or any other country to go out of its way to help Germany to export and to import. She was quite capable of looking after herself. Thanks to her novel trading methods, which were as unconventional as they were unscrupulous, she was well in a position to secure for herself a place in the sun. She elaborated an immense variety of methods by which she was able to trick other countries into increasing their trade with her whether they liked it or not. Before 1914, and again between the end of the last war and the advent of the Nazi régime, Germany was able to

expand her foreign trade largely with the aid of hard
and honest work. It is true there were from time to
time many complaints about subsidies and unfair competition through the offer of unsound long credits.
Generally speaking, however, Germany was able to
expand her exports because she was able to produce
cheap goods and to adapt her production to the
requirements of foreign buyers. After the advent of
the Nazi régime totally different methods were resorted
to. Germany no longer sought to maintain and increase her imports by underselling her competitors
abroad. She adopted the practice of concentrating
upon an effort to increase her purchases abroad and
to run up a big commercial indebtedness. And since
the only way in which she was able to settle such
debts was by means of exporting to the countries
concerned, it became necessary for the latter to
increase their purchases of German goods. The tortuous brains of German arch-conjurers invented an
immense variety of ways in which this end could be
achieved. For a detailed description of these methods
I must refer the reader to my book *Bloodless Invasion*
which appeared in 1938. It gives an account of the
Nazification of German commercial morality.

As I have already said, for Germans in general
honesty is not a matter of ethics but a matter of
expediency. From a purely practical point of view
it was more important for the German Government
to secure the maximum of raw materials required for
rearmament than to maintain the goodwill created
abroad by generations of German merchants who
considered it to their advantage to be honest in their
dealings with foreign importers. Owing to the preoccupation of German industries with rearmament

and the shortage of labour and good raw material that was developing during the last few pre-war years, it was not possible to maintain the quality of German manufactures. The use of inferior substitutes and slipshod workmanship resulted in a marked deterioration which in normal conditions would have meant the loss of many markets abroad. In order to be able to maintain these markets and even expand them, Germany resorted to fraudulent practices as a result of which countries in South-Eastern Europe, and to a less extent in many other parts of the world, had to buy these German goods even if they were inferior in quality or more expensive than their rival British products. Since large frozen reichsmark balances became accumulated on the clearing account of these countries with Germany, and since these balances could not be liquidated otherwise than through the purchase of German goods, the Governments concerned felt compelled to encourage the purchase of various kinds of unnecessary German products or of useful products in unnecessarily large quantities. In fact Germany was only prepared to sell to her South-Eastern European creditors goods which she was unable to sell for cash in other countries. The Danube Basin and the Balkans became Germany's happy dumping-ground. Several countries of South-Eastern Europe bought up hundreds of thousands of German mouth-organs and huge quantities of aspirins, not to speak of antiquated models of typewriters, cheap wireless sets which they themselves could well produce, second-hand motor cars, etc. If these countries wanted to buy something which Germany was reluctant to sell them, all she had to do was to put up the price and make it prohibitive for the unwanted buyers.

Germany embarked systematically upon spoiling the non-German markets of the South-Eastern European countries. She resold abroad part of the products bought from them at a considerable loss, partly for the sake of obtaining free exchange for goods bought on a credit basis, and partly in order to make it impossible for the South-Eastern European countries to export to any markets other than Germany.

For a long time, British opinion took very little notice of the German penetration in South-Eastern Europe. Indeed, many of those who did take notice, actually favoured German expansion in that part of the world. The *mea culpa* school argued that since the Ottawa Agreement excluded Germany from British markets, it was only natural that she should compensate herself by securing the monopoly in markets and raw material resources in the Continent in general, and in South-Eastern Europe in particular. As a matter of fact we shall see in Chapters VIII and IX that the effect of the Ottawa Agreement on German export trade was not nearly so pronounced as its opponents would like us to believe. Germany would have been well in a position to cover her normal import requirements with the aid of her exports even without securing monopoly over South-Eastern Europe, had it not been for the fact that her rearmament artificially increased her requirements. She wanted to have guns *and* butter, and it was for that purpose that she needed her monopoly in South-Eastern Europe.

The German trade drive had, however, also another object. By securing trade monopoly, Germany sought to secure political influence in South-Eastern Europe. In fact, she abused her strong economic position in various Danubian countries. In several known instances German diplomatic representatives or trade negotiators brought pressure to bear on these countries to drop certain members of their Governments who were not sufficiently friendly towards Germany. The outstanding example of political blackmail, based on trade monopoly, was the insistence on the part of the German Minister in Budapest, in 1938, that a book criticising Germany should be suppressed.

Another characteristic instance of the variety of conjuring tricks developed by the tortuous brains of Berlin was the granting of long-term credits to importers in South-Eastern Europe. It has always been a favourite device of Germany to be generous with her credit terms in her export trade, at the expense of other countries. Before 1931, and even before 1914, it had been a well-established practice for German exporters to outbid their rivals by offering long credits and to finance these transactions by means of short-term loans from London and other centres. After 1931 this was no longer possible, even though certain quarters in the City were doing their best to revive the practice to some extent almost to the eve of war. Germany then resorted to the method of financing her long-term credits at the expense of the borrowing countries themselves. This may sound paradoxical. Yet it was worked in a very simple fashion. On the basis of clearing agreements with South-Eastern European countries, German exporters were paid out of the proceeds of German imports from the same countries. Since the trade balance was in favour of Germany, the German exporters were able to collect their money irrespective of the long-term credits which they granted by order from official quarters. It was at the other end that the German long-term credits caused difficulties. Rumanian, Yugoslavian, etc., exporters to Germany were supposed to be paid out of the proceeds of German exports to Rumania, etc. If payment for these exports were deferred for four or five years it meant that the South-Eastern European exporters had to wait longer for their money. Since they could not afford to do this, they had to be accommodated by their Central Banks, so that these banks had to inflate credit in order to finance the German long-term credit transactions. The Hungarian Government had to comply because the Germans threatened to refuse the purchase of the Hungarian fruit crop, which could not possibly be sold at short notice to any other country.

After the *Anschluss*, Germany inherited Austria's share in South-Eastern European trade and her total participation thus reached an alarming proportion. She was well on her way to squeezing out other countries. That this was her object was frankly admitted. It was at this stage that interest in Great Britain began to awake. Although British trade with South-Eastern Europe was small, it was by no means negligible. Nevertheless, as we shall see in Chapter IX, certain political and industrial quarters were quite prepared to sacrifice it for the sake of appeasing Germany. It is to the credit of Mr. R. S. Hudson, then Secretary of the Department of Overseas Trade, to have launched the counter-offensive against the German trade drive in South-Eastern Europe. He was closely followed by Mr. Oliver Stanley, then President of the Board of Trade. Both Ministers made public statements criticising the methods applied by Germany in her trade with Danubian and Balkan countries and also in other countries. They succeeded in persuading Mr. Chamberlain in the late spring of 1938 to adopt a policy aiming at economic assistance to South-Eastern Europe, in order to save them from coming under German politico-economic control. It was one thing, however, to accept the principle and a totally different thing to put it into operation. The British counterblast to the German south-eastward trade thrust, as British action in so many other respects during the subsequent years, came too late, and when it did come it was inadequate. Indeed, it required an unusual degree of optimism (or alternatively a perverted sense of humour) to describe the supreme slow-motion picture of British economic assistance to South-Eastern Europe as a " British trade drive ". The British action would have been slow even if it had been unopposed from within and from without, because of the natural dislike of permanent officials for anything that is unconventional and unprece-dented. British assistance to South-Eastern Europe involved the departure from principles which have always been considered as sacrosanct in Whitehall. It meant the granting of credits to Governments which, from a purely commercial point of view, were not, strictly speaking, credit-worthy, apart from the political risk involved. It also meant the purchase of goods at prices above the world market level ; for if these countries had been able to sell their goods at world market level outside Germany, there would have been no need for any British action. Treasury and Board of Trade officials were horrified at the idea of embark-ing upon such unconventional action. It was contrary to their cherished traditions and they found it difficult

to adapt their minds to the new policy thrust upon
them by politicians. They were not in a position to
resist the policy imposed upon them from above, but
without having to depart from their normal routine
they were able to delay it by all the approved methods
of official procrastination and red-tape.

In addition to this obstacle, formidable enough in
itself, the so-called British trade drive met with
stubborn opposition on the part of the appeasement
school. There was of course a storm of indignation
in the German Press, and the *Berliner Boersenzeitung*
and other Nazi organs accused Great Britain of having
brought about the economic encirclement of Germany
long before a single transaction was concluded in
execution of the new policy. This German Press
campaign provided an opportunity for the British
appeasers to oppose the new policy on the ground
that it was irritating Germany. Sir John Simon (as
he then was) was doing his utmost to oppose the
adoption of the policy. Mr. Chamberlain, however,
decided in its favour.

The Treasury, however, was doing its utmost to
live up to its reputation as the chief bottle-neck
of Britain. During the course of the negotiations
with Turkey for credit and a trade agreement, the
Turkish delegates became so exasperated on several
occasions that they were on the point of returning to
Ankara and advising their Government to come to
terms with the German delegates who were waiting
on the doorstep. They found both Mr. S. D. Waley
and Sir Frederick Leith-Ross very difficult to deal
with.

Towards the end of May 1938, when negotiations
with the Turks threatened to come to a deadlock,

Mr. Chamberlain decided to take action and instructed the Treasury to conclude without further delay. At the same time it was also decided that Sir Frederick Leith-Ross should lead a British trade delegation to Rumania in order to discuss possibilities of economic and financial assistance. The departure of this delegation was, however, postponed until after the German occupation of Czecho-Slovakia in March 1939. When it eventually did materialise, the result of the prolonged labour of the mountain was the birth of a mouse. A loan of some £5 million was granted with some difficulty. Admittedly, in the light of subsequent events it is fortunate that a larger amount was not wasted upon Rumania. But this could not have been foreseen by the Treasury officials concerned. Moreover, they were even more tight-fisted in relation to Greece, which country only received £2 million. In the light of subsequent events it is now evident that it would have been to the advantage of this country to grant her a much larger amount. Conceivably the initial possession of superior equipment might have enabled the Greek Army to drive the Italians into the sea before they had a chance of consolidating a front in Albania. On balance, therefore, it would have been beneficial if the Treasury had been less tight-fisted, even if it would have meant a bigger dead loss in Rumania.

After the Munich surrender appeasement reigned supreme. It looked as if the policy of economic assistance to South-Eastern Europe had been dropped before its execution had even begun. Two members of the Government went out of their way to state that Germany should be allowed a free hand in South-Eastern Europe. One of them went so far as to say that Germany should be assisted in expanding her trade in that part of the world — a patronising remark which earned a well-deserved rebuke on the part of the German Press, which stated that Germany was not in need of British assistance in her trade drive in South-Eastern Europe. It was all the more surprising when in October 1938 the Government decided to make a purchase of 200,000 tons of Rumanian wheat. Although the amount involved was small, the gesture was significant and constituted a first-rate defeat for the appeasement school. Indeed, it was the first indication pointing towards a reversal of the policy of Munich.

CHAPTER VIII

ALTHOUGH the subject of this chapter has repeatedly been touched upon in the last two chapters, it is worth discussing in detail, because the conclusion of the trade agreement in 1934 constituted the first major act of economic appeasement. By the time of its conclusion it was generally known that Germany was rearming rapidly, and that she would soon become a menace to European peace. The development of the German Air Force under Goering was making rapid headway, and stories such as that of the manufacturing of machine-guns in perambulator factories received ample confirmation. The Nazi movement in Austria was receiving heavy subsidies from Germany. Large amounts were spent on the import of raw materials for rearmament, and also on propaganda abroad. Rearmament and public works undertaken on a gigantic scale were largely responsible for the unfavourable change in the German trade balance. The speeches of Hitler and other Nazi leaders were becoming increasingly aggressive, and the vituperations of the German Press against Great Britain and other democratic countries increasingly offensive. Evidently one would have thought that this was not the moment for initiating a policy of economic appeasement.

1934 was a critical year for the Nazi régime. Economic conditions in Germany were far from satisfactory, and the reckless expenditure of the Government was viewed with growing distrust. There was a great deal of criticism within the Nazi Party, but the spirit of opposition was stamped out ruthlessly by the Blood Purge of June 30. Had it not been for the moral and material effect of the Anglo-German trade agreement which was concluded at about the same time, it is conceivable that the Nazi régime might have collapsed. Admittedly, the chances are that it would have survived even in the absence of this act of economic appeasement, but it is certain that the progress of German rearmament would have been much slower.

It is true that in concluding the agreement the Treasury was guided in part at least by a desire to safeguard the interests of British creditors of Germany. There were, in the first place, the holders of the Dawes and Young Loans, who had every right to claim that the Treasury was morally responsible for the bonds issued under official auspices. There were also the British exporters, who were unable to obtain payment from Germany. The arrears of this kind amounted to several millions of pounds. There were also the holders of sundry long-term bonds issued by the German local authorities or industrial undertakings. Last but not least, there were the banking creditors. The Treasury, realising its moral responsibility, secured satisfactory terms for the Dawes and Young Loans. The Government also insisted upon terms which secured the repayment of commercial arrears during a comparatively brief period. The remaining categories of creditors, however, were left to the mercy of the German Government. The long-term creditors had to be satisfied with interest payment in the form of special bonds, and only the interest on interest due to them was paid in foreign currency. Nor were the rights of the banking creditors safeguarded.

The right solution would have been to establish compulsory exchange clearing and to make sure that Germany did not import an excessive amount of raw materials. The clearing could have provided for all categories of creditors without leaving for Germany any surplus in free sterling. As a matter of fact, simultaneously with the conclusion of the Anglo-German Trade and Payments Agreement, a Clearing Agreement was also concluded and initiated on the understanding that, should the Payments Agreement break down, the Clearing Agreement would become operative.

During the summer and autumn of 1934 it looked as if the Payments Agreement would not survive. Its terms had to be changed on two occasions, as the arrangements did not appear to have worked satisfactorily. At one time in November 1934 it looked as though the arrangement was on the verge of breakdown. At this stage, however, Mr. Montagu Norman and the Bank of England stepped in. An advance of £750,000 was granted to the Reichsbank to enable the latter to tide over the difficult period. The Payments Agreement was saved, and the adoption of exchange clearing was obviated. The granting of the loan of £750,000 was one of the outstanding acts of economic appeasement for which Mr. Montagu Norman was responsible. The result was that the Payments Agreement continued and secured immense advantages to Germany during subsequent years.

Admittedly, until the early part of 1936 the German

export surplus to Great Britain was used for the repayment of British commercial arrears. Even so, the terms of the agreement were highly beneficial for Germany, since she exported to this country mostly manufactures which were not indispensable for Great Britain, while she imported from this country mostly raw materials utilised for rearmament. It was from 1936 onwards that the agreement of 1934 began to produce its full results. When the repayment of the commercial arrears was completed, it was expected that the sterling surplus, which became henceforth available, would be allocated to the other classes of British creditors of Germany. It was hoped that the terms granted to long-term creditors would be improved, and that banking creditors under the Standstill Agreement would receive some capital repayments. Instead the sterling surplus was left at Germany's free disposal. It amounted to many millions of pounds year after year. During the period between October 1, 1934, and March 31, 1939, the free sterling surplus representing the difference between German exports to Great Britain and British exports to Germany amounted to £55,446,000. Of this amount rather less than £20 million was used for the service of Germany's various debts to Great Britain, leaving rather more than £35 million at Germany's disposal. A large part of this amount was spent on raw materials, but even the £89,676,000 of Germany's purchases from Great Britain consisted largely of raw materials. The total raw materials purchased by Germany with the aid of the proceeds of her exports to Great Britain under the Anglo-German Trade and Payments Agreement of 1934 amounted to at least £100 million. Considering that raw materials as a rule constitute one-tenth or less of the value of war materials for whose production they are used, it is easy to imagine the extent to which the Anglo-German agreement assisted Germany in her spectacular rearmament drive.

From 1936 onwards there were frequent protests in the Press and Parliament against the one-sided advantages Germany enjoyed from the working of the agreement of 1934. By that time it was impossible to overlook the aggressive intentions of the Third Reich. In 1936 Germany remilitarised the Rhineland, contrary to the terms of the Locarno Pact. She also violated other pledges given, and her intervention in the Spanish Civil War showed that her growing strength was becoming a grave menace to peace. Even those who failed to realise in 1934 that Nazi Germany was becoming the Public Enemy Number One of Europe must have become aware of that fact two years later. There was simply no excuse for continuing to subsidise German rearmament.

In spite of this the agitation in favour of terminating or changing the agreement of 1934 was persistently ignored by the Government. By that time the philosophy of appeasement, which only existed sub-consciously and in an embryonic form in 1934, became the deliberately adopted creed of an influential section of British politicians, Government officials and news-papers. One of the characteristic arguments used in defence of the agreement of 1934 was that Germany spent a large part of her free sterling surplus on British re-exports. Since, however, these re-exports were constituted of raw materials which Germany needed, there was little to be said in favour of that argument. After all, the extent to which the London commercial and financial centre benefited by these re-exports represented only a small fraction of the amount involved. Very few of those who were in favour of continuing the agreement of 1934 had the honesty to admit that the reason for their attitude was their fear that if Great Britain were to deprive Germany of the advantages she enjoyed she would be driven into pursuing a more aggressive foreign policy. As a matter of fact, German foreign policy in 1936 and 1937 was as aggressive as it could possibly be at that stage of the progress of German rearmament.

Admittedly, the whole of the proceeds of Germany's exports to Great Britain was not used for war purposes. A large part of it paid for food, raw materials and manufactures for civilian requirements. Even that part, however, contributed indirectly towards assisting German rearmament. After all, Goering's " Guns instead of butter " policy was never enforced to the letter. Had it been too rigidly enforced, the discontent of the civilian population would have undermined the stability of the National Socialist régime. The Anglo-German Trade and Payments Agreement went a long way towards enabling the Nazi régime to obtain guns as well as a certain amount of butter, sufficient to keep the population reasonably content.

The figures of the Anglo-German visible trade balance did not in any way indicate the full extent to which Germany benefited by the one-sided advantages granted to her. The system in operation was even more one-sidedly in Germany's favour as far as invisible trade items are concerned. While Germany allowed practically no exchange for German visitors to Great Britain, she derived a considerable income from British tourist traffic in Germany. It is true the greater part of the tourists' spendings was

H

effected in "travel marks", whose proceeds served mainly for the repayment of short-term Standstill creditors. Since, however, the maximum of travel marks authorised per person per day was limited, many tourists exceeded that limit, and Germany obtained a by no means inconsiderable net influx of foreign exchange as a result of the British tourist traffic. This must be so, otherwise the German authorities would not have made such an effort to attract tourists, with the aid of posters inviting Englishmen to "come to see Mediaeval Germany". If the tourist traffic had been solely for the benefit of foreign creditors, the German authorities would not have gone out of their way to stimulate it.

The agreement of 1934 made no provisions for the payment of freights. Consequently Germany laid down rules which secured for her unilateral advantages. If anyone sent a consignment of goods from Germany to Great Britain, he was only allowed to pay the freight in reichsmarks up to the German frontier. Any freight beyond the German frontiers was payable by the British importer in foreign currencies. On the other hand, if a British exporter sent goods to Germany, the freight was paid in sterling for the whole route, and Germany's share of the freight (port dues, railway freight, etc.) was collected therefore in sterling.

German companies with subsidiary companies in Great Britain were entitled to repatriate their profits in full in the form of free sterling. British companies having subsidiaries in Germany, on the other hand, had to accumulate their profits in the form of blocked marks.

Any sums inherited from British residents by

residents in Germany could be transferred direct and swell the foreign exchange reserves of the Reichsbank. On the other hand, residents in Great Britain could only collect legacies in Germany in the form of blocked marks.

German authors, playwrights, composers, etc., collected their royalties in Great Britain in free sterling. On the other hand, their British colleagues had to be satisfied with blocked marks for their German royalties.

These are only a few characteristic instances indicating the grossly unfair and one-sided system which was allowed to exist. The Government was fully aware of it ; various interests concerned made repeated representations, but without any result. Even when in 1938 the agreement of 1934 was revised, these one-sided advantages in favour of Germany were allowed to stand.

The worst of it is that Germany failed to show the least appreciation of the extremely favourable terms she received from Great Britain. The German Press incessantly showered torrents of abuse on Great Britain and consistently accused the British Government of economic encirclement. German politicians and journalists had exhausted their vocabulary of invective in their anti-British outbursts, so that they could not possibly have been more offensive and abusive even if all the advantages Germany enjoyed had been withdrawn. Evidently the policy of appeasement did not buy any goodwill and did not generate any conciliatory spirit in Germany.

In addition to the direct assistance provided by the one-sided character of the agreement of 1934, Germany also derived considerable indirect assistance from Great Britain as a result of the easy-going British foreign trade policy. Every one of the States of Northern Europe had a very large favourable trade balance in relation to Great Britain. On the other hand, their trade with Germany was more or less evenly balanced on the basis of the exchange clearing agreements with Germany. This means that since they could sell as much as they liked to Great Britain without having to buy an equivalent amount of British goods, while they were unable to sell to Germany unless they bought German manufactures in return, it was to their advantage to divert orders from British to German manufactures. Germany would not have been able to buy so much Swedish iron ore for rearmament, or Bofors guns, had it not been for the fact that Great Britain made no serious efforts to induce Sweden to spend on British goods a larger part of the proceeds of her sales in Great Britain. British and German industries were more or less competitive. While the price of subsidised German manufactures may have been lower, their quality was usually inferior, especially as, owing to raw-material shortage and the preoccupation of German industries with rearmament, bad substitutes were used and there was a great deal of hasty and careless workmanship in the production of manufactures. If only Great Britain had insisted upon a higher degree of bilateralism in her trade with Northern European countries, Germany would never have been able to rearm on anything like the scale she has rearmed.

The free exchange obtained by Germany out of the proceeds of her visible and invisible exports to Great Britain helped her in her rearmament drive far in excess of the actual amount involved. It constituted a very large part of the free exchange at her disposal and it gave her the benefit of a certain degree of elasticity in her foreign trade operations. In the absence of the free exchange obtained through Great Britain there would have been frequent stoppages in the German rearmament drive, for it would have been impossible to secure the continuity of raw-material supplies. From time to time the makers of guns and aeroplanes would have had to wait until the proceeds of German exports enabled Germany to import from Latin America or Canada the corresponding amount of the materials they urgently required. It was for filling such gaps that the Danegeld paid by Great Britain in the form of free sterling came in extremely useful.

Those who were responsible for the conclusion of the Anglo-German Trade and Payments Agreement of 1934 incurred grave responsibility for the war. Had it not been for their shortsightedness and gross error of judgment, Germany would never have been able to destroy the independence of a number of nations within the brief space of three years. Admittedly, it is easy to be wise after the event, but there were many critics of the Government's policy who foresaw and foretold the disastrous consequences of the agreement of 1934 and whose warnings then and in subsequent years were persistently ignored. Nor could these critics be blamed if they could not resist the temptation of deriving melancholy satisfaction out of reminding the adherents of the school of appeasement that their policy did not work. Even after the experience of Munich and Prague, Germany was left in full possession of the advantages obtained from the agreement of 1934. The modification of that agreement in June 1938 and the unfavourable change in the German trade balance owing to the growing spontaneous boycott of

German goods by the British public did not wipe out these advantages, even though they became reduced to some extent. Any suggestion of a revision of the agreement to secure reciprocity for British interests, and especially a fair deal for British creditors, was met with the argument that Germany would interpret such a move as an unfriendly act, which had to be avoided at all costs. Rather than incur Berlin's displeasure, Great Britain continued to pay Germany Danegeld in the form of a free sterling exchange surplus on Anglo-German trade and in various other forms, until the very eve of the war.

CHAPTER IX

THE DÜSSELDORF DEAL

SOUTH-EASTERN EUROPE was by no means the only sphere in which German economic penetration was making progress. Indeed, while Germany was complaining bitterly about economic encirclement her trade was gaining ground in various countries in Northern Europe, in the traditional British markets of Latin America and even in certain parts of the British Empire. The methods applied in these various markets differed from those successfully applied in South-Eastern Europe. Nevertheless, they were all variations on the theme of currency fraud and trade conjuring tricks.

In December 1938 Mr. Hudson — who, as we saw, was largely responsible for the initiation of the policy of British assistance to South-Eastern Europe — made a strong speech condemning German trading methods in general. He declared that unless Germany was prepared to modify her trading methods and refrain from unfair competition Great Britain would beat her at her own game. The language used, coming as it did barely two months after the Munich surrender, was surprisingly firm and created consternation in the camp of appeasers. The German Ambassador, Herr von Dirksen, hastened to call on Sir Horace Wilson at 10 Downing Street to lodge a complaint against this official statement. Purely as a matter of form he also

sent one of his junior Secretaries to the (official)
Foreign Office across the road to register his complaint.
It was widely expected that Mr. Hudson's bold state-
ment would cost him his office.

As a matter of fact, the response of the British
Press was very favourable. After the humiliation of
Munich and the subsequent months, firm language on
the part of a member of the Government was almost
unanimously welcomed. Consequently he remained a
member of the Government. His attitude was fully
endorsed by his immediate chief, Mr. Stanley, who in
a subsequent statement crossed the " *t*'s " and dotted
the " *i*'s " of Mr. Hudson's challenge to Germany.
All that remained was to follow up the words by
action.

Before anything could happen, however, there was
a minor crisis in the Government. Mr. Hudson and
two other junior Ministers, encouraged by his success,
delivered an ultimatum to No. 10 Downing Street
demanding the dismissal of several senior Ministers
whom they considered inefficient from the point of
view of the arms drive. To give their move more
weight, they tendered their resignation. Mr. Chamberlain kept them waiting for about a fortnight before
taking his decision, which was one of compromise.
One of the senior Ministers, Sir Thomas Inskip, whose
head was demanded, was dropped, but the resignation
of one of the three rebel junior Ministers was accepted.
Following upon a visit at No. 10, Mr. Hudson with-
drew his resignation. Nobody knows what happened
at his conversation with Mr. Chamberlain, but following upon his conversation he changed his policy.
He abandoned his demand for a counterblast to the
German trade drive in South-Eastern Europe or else-

where, and ranged himself in favour of a policy of economic appeasement.[1]

During the early months of 1939 an effort was made to come to an arrangement with Germany by means of direct negotiations between British and German industries. The object of this attempt as originally stated was supposed to be to safeguard the interests of British trade against the unfair methods of competition denounced by Mr. Hudson and Mr. Stanley. It was supposed to be an eleventh-hour attempt to avert the trade war foreshadowed by those two Ministers in case of Germany's refusal to modify her trading methods.

Those methods placed the British industries at a great disadvantage well outside the territories which Germany claimed for herself as her *Lebensraum*. Indeed, the very fact that German trade penetration was making such good progress in Latin America and in British Dominions showed the utter falsity of the *Lebensraum* doctrine from an economic point of view. Notwithstanding trade barriers and other difficulties, Germany was able until the very eve of the war to maintain and even expand her trade positions in any part of the world. There would have been some economic justification for her claim for control over Continental markets if she had been excluded from overseas markets. This was, however, by no means the case. It is repeated to boredom that as a result of the Ottawa Agreement Germany was compelled to

---

[1] In all fairness to Mr. Hudson, it must be admitted that much credit is due to him for the initiation of the anti-appeasement drive, so that in spite of his subsequent *volte-face* there is a net credit balance in his favour on his political balance-sheet. Moreover, after the outbreak of the war he rendered valuable services both as Secretary to the Department of Overseas Trade and as Minister of Agriculture.

seek the control of South-Eastern Europe because she was excluded from the British Empire. This argument received powerful support by the free-trader section of British economists, which could never forgive Great Britain for the Ottawa Agreement. These economists may dislike Hitler, but their feeling towards him is positively mild compared with their violent hatred of British supporters of protectionism or Imperial preference. They readily supply Dr. Goebbels with raw material for anti-British propaganda by denouncing the Ottawa Agreement as the true villain of the piece.

The true state of affairs in this respect is clearly indicated by the following instance. Early in 1939 the municipality of Cape Town invited tenders for certain important public works. Although the German tender was lower than the British tender it was decided to accept the latter. Thereupon the German Minister in South Africa lodged a complaint with the Government of the Union, and General Hertzog sternly reprimanded the municipal authorities, threatening them with action unless they modified their decision. This attitude, which earned the South African Prime Minister the nickname of " Gauleiter Hertzog " in the British Press, shows the degree of politico-economic influence achieved by Germany in one of the British Dominions. Apart from political considerations which may have played a part in inducing General Hertzog to take such a strange line, his attitude was largely the result of the skilful trade policy pursued by Germany in South Africa. For several years the Germans bought up a very large proportion of South Africa's wool and to a large extent acquired virtual control of the wool trade. The prices the German buyers paid were somewhat above the world market level. In order to secure payment, however, it became necessary for South Africa to increase her imports of German manufactures. As a result British exporters suffered disadvantage. It was in order to balance trade between the two countries that General Hertzog insisted upon the acceptance of the German tender by the Cape Town municipal council.

South Africa was by no means the only British Dominion in which Germany succeeded in securing a foothold. Important barter agreements were concluded also with Australia. In various Latin-American States, too, Germany was gaining ground through the application of the aski mark system, which is an ingenious variation of the clearing system applied in South-Eastern Europe.

British trade, already handicapped by an overvaluation of the pound in relation to the dollar, was losing ground in face of the onslaught by German exporters. It was hoped that as a result of the negotiations initiated by the Federation of British Industries their interests would be adequately safeguarded, or that alternatively, in case of a breakdown of these negotiations, they would receive from their Government the same support which their German rivals receive from the German Government.

Before long, however, it became evident that what was originally intended to be a trade drive directed against Germany's trading methods was becoming a movement flavouring distinctly of appeasement. The circumstances in which it was given an appeasement twist are impossible to ascertain. The fact is that in January and February 1939 little was said and even less was done about beating Germany with her own weapons in international trade competition. Instead politicians and industrialists embarked upon an attempt at devising methods by which Germany could be enabled to increase her exports.

Conceivably the explanation why the British trade drive went wrong lies in Hitler's Reichstag speech of January 30, 1939. He was generally expected to deliver one of his usual vitriolic onslaughts against Great Britain, reinforced with threats. The world was relieved to find that his tone was unexpectedly moderate. There was only one point on which he laid stress and that was Germany's foreign trade requirements. He declared " Germany must export or die ", and threatened Great Britain with sweeping reprisals if she should make efforts to gain ground in foreign markets at Germany's expense. Since the speech did not foreshadow any aggressive act in the political sphere, the appeasement school triumphantly pointed out that Hitler was now quite prepared to follow a reasonable foreign policy provided that Germany was allowed to export in accordance with her vital requirements. Accordingly the appeasement school, supported effectively by Mr. Hudson, set out to satisfy Hitler in this respect. They endeavoured to devise a scheme to enable Germany to increase her exports without thereby hurting British interests. The fact that negotiations were confined to representatives of British and German industries to the exclusion of other industries gave rise to suspicion that the object was to strike a bargain which would secure advantages for Germany at the expense of other industrial countries which were not represented at these negotiations.

The Federation of British Industries lent itself willingly to what was mainly a political manœuvre in the interest of appeasement. Admittedly, there was a possibility that certain British industries might secure for themselves advantages through a bargain with German industries. It was very difficult to see, however, what advantages British trade as a whole could possibly have derived from an agreement with German industries as a whole. The basic fact of the situation was that Germany had exchange clearing agreements or other forms of semi-barter arrangements with the predominant majority of foreign countries, and that the countries which supplied her with goods could only obtain payment by importing German goods in return. Since it was utterly unlikely that Germany intended to reduce her imports from any of the countries concerned, it stood to reason that she had to maintain her exports. It was most unlikely, for instance, that Germany contemplated a reduction of her imports of iron ore from Sweden or of wool from South Africa. This being so, it was inevitable that, irrespective of any agreement with the British industrialists, she would have to continue exporting goods to Sweden and to South Africa to the same total value as before. It was conceivable that Germany would be prepared to reduce her exports of, say, motor cars or electrical equipments to South Africa in return for similar concessions on the part of the corresponding British industries in South-Eastern Europe. The trouble was that it was impossible to include in the arrangement all British industries. Only a small number of important industries were in a position to negotiate such agreements with Germany. And since Germany was determined to continue importing South African wool on the same scale as before, an agreement with half a dozen or a dozen British industries to refrain from competing with them in South Africa would only have meant an increase in German competition with the remaining two hundred-odd minor British industries interested in exports to South Africa. British trade as a whole would not have benefited, for the gain of the major industries would have been offset by the loss of the minor industries.

Let us take another example. By virtue of the German-Swedish payments agreement, trade between the two countries had to balance. If Germany agreed to a reduction of her exports to Sweden, it would have meant that she would have had to import less iron ore for her rearmament, arsenic for poison gas and other useful and indispensable materials. It is hardly conceivable that Germany would have agreed to do it. She would have wanted to keep up the total volume of her imports from Sweden, and to that end she would have had to keep up the total volume of her exports to that country, even if she had agreed to changes within the limits of the grand total. As in the case of South Africa, the gains of the British industries which were represented at the negotiations would have been the losses of those British industries which were not represented.

Needless to say, it would have taken something like six months or more after the conclusion of an agreement for the British interests concerned and the British public to realise the truth of this. In the meantime the agreement between British and German industries would have been hailed as a triumph for economic appeasement and would have served as a basis for further major acts of political as well as economic appeasement.

The favourite formula in the camp of appeasers

was, of course, that this country should disinterest itself in South-Eastern Europe in return for concessions from Germany in other parts of the world. Needless to say, there was not the slightest chance of a compromise on such lines since Hitler already considered South-Eastern Europe as his special preserve and would not have been prepared to make any sacrifices elsewhere for the sake of South-Eastern European trade, which he was well on his way towards capturing in any case. The deal would have met with strong opposition also in British political circles. Mr. Chamberlain himself was in favour of maintaining and if possible increasing British trade with South-Eastern Europe. Any bargain which would have meant the abandonment of South-Eastern Europe to the mercy of Germany would have aroused a storm of indignation in Parliament and in the country. That was the reason why the appeasers sought to cover the political gesture of *désintéressement* in South-Eastern Europe under the disguise of an apparently non-political agreement between industries.

Fate and Hitler willed it otherwise. When after the preliminary discussions in Berlin the representatives of the Federation of British Industries and the Reichsgruppe Industrie met at Düsseldorf in March 1939 (a meeting-place which was agreed upon in preference to Godesberg, tactfully suggested by the Germans), the Czecho-Slovak crisis was already approaching its climax. It was obvious that, notwithstanding official sunshine talk, storm clouds were gathering on the horizon. Germany was stirring up trouble in Slovakia and was making preparations to fish in troubled waters. This did not, however, prevent the British industries concerned from settling down to discussions with their German colleagues at Düsseldorf. Arrangements were made for the opening of the full conference in Berlin in the near future. Mr. Stanley and Mr. Hudson accepted invitations to a dinner to be arranged in their honour on the occasion of the opening of this conference.

All the time, however, the Government was at pains to emphasise that the negotiations were purely a matter for the industrialists themselves and that the Government itself would keep aloof. This formula was highly suitable for the purposes of appeasement, since it gave the Government a chance to deal with Germany through the intermediary of the industrialists without having to assume responsibility for the deal before Parliament.

A few days after the opening of the Düsseldorf negotiations, however, the Czecho-Slovak crisis entered its decisive phase. German troops crossed the frontier a few hours before the unfortunate Czech President, Dr. Hacha, was forced to fix his signature on the dotted line of an agreement in Berlin surrendering his country to Germany. Hitler had broken his pledge given at Munich to Mr. Chamberlain.

One should have thought that this was not the moment for entering into a new agreement with Germany. Apart altogether from the moral aspects of shaking hands with the aggressor immediately after he had committed his latest act of aggression, it was, to say the least, doubtful whether any undertaking given on the day after the previous undertaking was broken would be of any practical value. Indeed, when the news of the occupation of Czecho-Slovakia reached the negotiators at Düsseldorf, the German industrialists fully expected that the conference would be

broken off. After consultation with London, however,
the delegates astonished their German colleagues by
announcing their intention of proceeding with the
matter and signing the hastily drafted preliminary
agreement. It was actually signed on the day when
Hitler made his triumphal entry into German-occupied
Prague. There is every reason to suppose that the
British delegates would not have signed the agreement without having been told to do so by the
Government.

The indignation aroused in Great Britain and in
other democratic countries by the news of the conclusion of the Düsseldorf agreement became further
accentuated when the details of the deal were
announced. Even though the agreement only contained the outlines of the fundamental principles
upon which future agreements to be negotiated
directly between individual industries were to be
based, it was sufficient to indicate the true character
of the deal. One of the clauses actually stated that
one of the objects of the agreement was to enable
Germany to increase her foreign exchange resources.
While the contracting parties disclaimed that the
agreement was directed against third parties, no
third country was actually invited to Düsseldorf or
to Berlin. Apparently the idea was that if any other
countries should wish to participate by signing on the
dotted line they were at liberty to do so. The alternative they had to face was a threat of Anglo-German
industrial co-operation to fight their competition.
Now the usual practice in international negotiations
is that the representatives of all leading countries
come together, and after they have reached an agreement they invite the countries of secondary import-

ance to adhere to the terms agreed upon. On this
occasion the contracting parties appeared to have
expected first-rate industrial countries simply to
accept the terms laid down between Great Britain
and Germany, in order to avoid a joint trade offensive
directed against them by British and German interests.
The idea was preposterous. The appeasement school
was, however, delighted. It was a great achievement
indeed to have succeeded in committing Great Britain
to a major act of appeasement on the day after
the bankruptcy of the whole policy was conclusively
proved by Hitler's invasion of Czecho-Slovakia.

There was, of course, no lack of criticism in the
Press and in the House of Commons. The attacks
directed against the Düsseldorf deal made it impossible
for the Government to uphold that agreement amidst
the atmosphere created by the occupation of Prague.
Rejoicing in the appeasement camp was thus short-
lived. Mr. Chamberlain, having stated on the day
of the German occupation of Prague that he had not
abandoned his determination to pursue the path of
appeasement, had to take a much stronger stand two
days later in a speech he delivered at Birmingham.
He declared that the Government was not dis-
interested in the fate of South-Eastern Europe.
Mr. Stanley and Mr. Hudson had to cancel their
dinner engagement in Berlin. Nevertheless, it was
hoped by appeasers that the storm of indignation
would blow over in a few weeks and that the industrial
negotiations could then be gradually resumed. As a
matter of fact, opposition to the trade pact remained
persistent and it became necessary to shelve the whole
scheme, for some time at any rate.

The terms of the Düsseldorf deal, the fact that it

was concluded on the day after the occupation of Prague, and the efforts to uphold it in spite of the evident failure of the appeasement policy, provide a characteristic example of the attitude of appeasers. They wanted to supply Germany with additional foreign exchange resources at the moment when German mechanised divisions were penetrating deep into Slovakia and were on the point of occupying Memel. Nobody knew at the time where those divisions would stop. It was widely believed that after the full conquest of Czecho-Slovakia the German armed forces would continue their triumphal march across Hungary and Rumania deep into the Balkans. The Hungarian and Rumanian armies were partially mobilised. In the north the surrender of Lithuania in the matter of Memel was considered to be merely the first step in another triumphal march. Yet at this very moment British politicians and industrialists were engaged in devising a scheme by which to enable Germany to accelerate her rearmament through increasing her foreign exchange resources.

As for the argument put forward by the apologists of the Düsseldorf agreement, that its completion would have led to an all-round increase of foreign trade which would have benefited all countries, it sounds utterly unconvincing. After all, the object of the agreement was the limitation of competition between manufacturing countries. This would have meant, of course, the charging of higher prices for manufactures. Considering that one of the main causes of the depression was the unduly low prices of agricultural products compared with manufacture prices, it is difficult to imagine how a further widening of this discrepancy could possibly have helped matters. Something must be wrong with the economics of a scheme which was based on the assumption that if in the absence of cut-throat competition higher prices are charged for manufactures, raw-material-producing countries would be able to buy more. Such minor inconsistencies disappear in significance, however, compared with the incredible political immorality and unwisdom of the proposed deal.

Although this act of appeasement was largely inspired by appeasement politicians, the industrialists and the Executive of the Federation of British Industries who lent themselves to that policy cannot escape blame. Their attitude and that of other members of the wealthy classes and high Society in Great Britain who constituted the mainstay of pro-German forces was simply beyond comprehension. It was a well-known fact that big German industrialists and the members of the *Herrenklub* who formerly constituted the ruling classes in Germany were anything but happy under the present régime. It is true strikes were outlawed. On the other hand, the Labour Front was incomparably more powerful than the trade unions had ever been under the Weimar Republic. To-day the German manufacturer is hardly more than a paid manager in his own works. Dividends are limited to a maximum of 6 or 8 per cent according to the case, and the proprietors have to put up with an immense amount of interference by the Labour Front, party organisations and the Government. They would be glad to change places with the British industrialists in spite of the latter's difficulties with trade unions. Nevertheless, British industrialists, or at any rate some of them, were eager to assist Nazi

Germany, judging by the conclusion of the Düsseldorf deal. It is no wonder David Low, in one of his immortal cartoons in the *Evening Standard*, drew the members of the British pro-Nazi " ruling classes " with donkeys' heads !

CHAPTER X

THE CZECH GOLD SCANDAL

AFTER the invasion of Austria the camp of appeasers was working overtime in finding excuses for the offence. It was argued that anyhow Austria was a bankrupt country and it was to her interest to be taken over; that this was in accordance with the wish of the majority of the Austrians; and that after the elimination of the most unjust clause of the Peace Treaty Hitler would now settle down to peaceful collaboration in Europe. These words of appeasement were supplemented by acts of appeasement. Immediately after the occupation of Vienna the Bank of England placed at the Reichsbank's disposal the assets it held on behalf of the Austrian National Bank. The Government took no steps to prevent this or to prevent the surrender of privately owned Austrian sterling assets to the German authorities. Accordingly gold and foreign exchange running into tens of millions of pounds fell into the hands of Germany.

From a legalistic point of view the surrender of the funds owned by the Austrian authorities was the logical outcome of the Government's decision to recognise the conquest. The legal position was not so clear regarding the balances owned by the Austrian National Bank which, after all, was a private concern. It is open to doubt whether the change in its management brought about through the arrest of its president, Dr. Kienboeck, was legally valid, and whether the

Bank of England was under legal obligation to carry out the instructions given by the National Bank under its new management. As for the privately owned assets, it was obvious that instructions for their surrender were given under duress and should not have been carried out. Even in the absence of any legislation or official request to that effect the London banks ought to have withheld these assets pending a legal decision. In many instances this was done, but in the absence of official guidance the majority of the banks surrendered the assets of their Austrian clients to Germany.

There was good reason to fear when Hitler followed up the invasion of Austria with the invasion of Czecho-Slovakia that the Czecho-Slovak foreign assets would meet with a similar fate. Fortunately this time the Government took a different attitude. Immediately after the occupation of Prague both official and private Czech assets were blocked. For once the Treasury acted swiftly, much to the astonishment of everybody, including the German authorities who were so perplexed by this unusual display of firmness that they even forgot to be offensive about it. The German Press took the line that the whole thing must be due to some curious misunderstanding that had arisen amidst the confusion, and that before long the situation would be cleared up and the Czech assets would be duly surrendered.

A substantial part of the Czech assets in London, however, fell into the invaders' hands. A gold deposit of about £6 million held by the Bank of England under the name of the Bank for International Settlements was surrendered upon instructions received from Prague. The circumstances of the surrender of this gold provided one of the most characteristic examples of financial appeasement. They deserve, therefore, close examination.

On March 15, a few hours after the entry of the German troops into Prague, a senior official of the Reichsbank, Herr Müller, accompanied by a number of minor officials, took charge of the Czecho-Slovak National Bank. One of his first instructions to the management was to surrender the bank's gold to the Reichsbank. Much to his disappointment he was informed that the amount of gold held actually in the bank's vault was negligible. It consisted mainly of the coins collected from the public during the crisis that preceded the Munich surrender. Practically the entire gold reserve was held in London, partly under the bank's own name and partly under the name of the Bank for International Settlements. Herr Müller thereupon ordered the management to instruct the Bank of England and the Bank for International Settlements to transfer the gold to the Reichsbank. For four days the executive of the National Bank did its utmost to delay complying with this order. The alternative to obeying was, however, confinement in a concentration camp. On March 19 it reluctantly complied with the German instructions under duress. By that time, however, the British authorities had taken steps to block the gold held in the National Bank's own name. The Bank of England refused to comply with the instructions received.

On the other hand, the Bank for International Settlements unhesitatingly surrendered the Czecho-Slovak National Bank's gold deposit to the Reichsbank. Responsibility for this decision rests with Dr. Beyen, who was then the head of the executive of the Bank for International Settlements. He over-ruled the objections of the French General Manager, M. Auboin, and in accordance with the insistent demands of the German Assistant General Manager, Herr Hechler, promptly took steps to instruct the Bank of England to transfer the gold to the Reichsbank. This was done in spite of the vigorous protest by M. Fournier, Governor of the Bank of France and a Director of the Bank for International Settlements, who was told by Dr. Beyen that as a Director he had no right even to ask for information on the matter.

M. Paul Reynaud, who was then French Finance Minister, took up the matter and received whole-hearted support from M. Bonnet, the then Foreign Minister. Although the latter was an appeaser him-self, in this matter he was certainly in favour of a firm attitude. Accordingly the question was raised through diplomatic channels and also on the occasion of President Lebrun's London visit. Notwithstanding this, the Treasury refused to take action. It did not even attempt to persuade Mr. Montagu Norman and Sir Otto Niemeyer, the two British Directors of the Bank for International Settlements, to support the French Directors in order to prevent the transfer of the gold. In the absence of pressure from Whitehall Mr. Norman and Sir Otto Niemeyer refrained from exerting their considerable influence at Basle to delay the transfer at least until the next meeting of the Board.

According to competent legal opinion the surrender of the gold by the Bank for International Settlements was entirely unjustified. It is the banking practice in Switzerland as in most other countries that if a banker has reason to believe that the instructions he

has received were given under duress, it is his right
and duty to refuse to comply. Law courts in Switzerland, as in many other countries, invariably rejected
during 1938 and 1939 the German attempts to seize
Austrian deposits abroad. The District Court of
Zurich passed a ruling to that effect on December 7,
1938, rejecting the claim of a Vienna banking house
for the transfer of its Swiss balance, on the ground
that its instructions were based upon law which was
not followed in Switzerland and was contrary to the
ordre publique Suisse. Dr. Beyen must have been
fully aware of this important ruling which was subsequently confirmed by the Court of Appeal. Notwithstanding this he took the line that under Swiss law
it was sufficient for him to satisfy himself that the
signatures on the letter containing the instructions
were in order, and that it was not his duty to inquire
whether those instructions were given under duress.
Yet even in the absence of specific inquiries, anyone
acquainted with the conditions prevailing in Prague
after the German occupation, when Czechs were
rounded up by the Gestapo by the thousand, must
have been aware that the surrender of the gold could
only possibly have been agreed upon under extreme
pressure.

In the complete absence of support on the part
of the British Directors the French Directors were
unable to prevent the surrender of the Czech gold.
On the occasion of the next Board Meeting of the
Bank for International Settlements in April 1939,
M. Fournier declared to Sir Otto Niemeyer, Chairman
of the Board, that he wished to place the matter on
the Agenda, whereupon he was told that it would
be of little use since 80 per cent of the gold had

already actually been transferred. The Directors agreed to wash their hands of the affair and regard it as a matter the settlement of which was within the competence of the Executive.

Those responsible for the surrender of the gold considered it advisable to take elaborate steps to avoid publicity and to cover the tracks of the transfer, which was carried out in such a way as to attract the least possible attention. The British Customs Returns disclosed no gold shipment to Germany in March or April 1939, and it is understood that the bars which eventually reached the Reichsbank were not identical with those which were held by the Bank for International Settlements on account of the Czecho-Slovak National Bank. Notwithstanding all the secrecy with which the whole affair was surrounded it became public two months later.

Meanwhile a German delegation arrived in London towards the middle of May, in order to discuss the question of blocked Czech assets. The Treasury was quite willing to discuss the matter. Having for once lapsed from its consistent attitude of appeasement on March 15 by blocking these assets, it was anxious to make good this " mistake " and to regularise the status of the blocked funds. Lord Simon, with his essentially legalistic mind, must have found it embarrassing to have committed himself to an action which, however justified it may be from a moral and political point of view, was open to question from a purely technical legal point of view. Senior officials of the Treasury felt in the same way, and consequently the Treasury was quite prepared to release in favour of Germany a large part of the blocked assets, provided that the German Government in turn was prepared to give its approval for the retention of the rest for the purpose of satisfying British claims against Czecho-Slovakia.

It was in order to come to some such compromise that the German delegation, headed by Herr Rüter, came to London. Its discussions were surrounded by an unusual degree of secrecy. As a rule the arrival of a foreign delegation of such importance is announced in the Press of both countries. In the present instance, however, no announcement was made either in Berlin or in London. Moreover, the members of the delegation were instructed to remain incognito as far as possible. They even refrained from establishing contact with their personal friends in London, and the staff of the hotel where they were staying was instructed to deny their presence in case of inquiries. Nevertheless, somehow it transpired within a day or two that secret negotiations were being pursued.

Some confusion was created by the report that Herr Wohltat was expected to come to London later to attend an international whaling conference. Certain quarters gained the impression that it was he who headed the mysterious German delegation which was already here. To clear up the mystery Mr. Duncan Sandys put down a question to the Chancellor of the Exchequer asking him whether it was true that negotiations were being concluded for the release of the blocked Czech assets. The question was to be asked on May 18, but Mr. Sandys was persuaded to withdraw his question.

On the same day, however, the *Financial News* published a news item stating that negotiations for the release of blocked Czech assets were being pursued and that Czech gold held by the Bank of England in

the name of the Bank for International Settlements
had actually been surrendered. This was the first
information about the gold transaction which was to
gain immense notoriety during the following weeks.
On May 19 the *Financial News* gave further details
of the surrender of the Czech gold by the Bank for
International Settlements. On the same day the
Daily Telegraph also published a news story which,
however, contained several inaccuracies of detail. It
gave publicity to the rumour that the German delegation in London was headed by Herr Wohltat, and
stated that the Czech gold held in the name of the
Bank for International Settlements had been released
by the Treasury.

On the same day Mr. Lloyd George raised the
matter during the course of the Foreign Affairs debate
in the House of Commons. He based his remarks on
the version published in the *Daily Telegraph*. Mr.
Chamberlain stated in his reply that Mr. Lloyd George
could set his mind at rest as " the whole story is a
mare's-nest ".

Now the generally accepted meaning of the term
" mare's-nest " is that the story which is described
as such is entirely devoid of foundation. In the
present instance Mr. Lloyd George's statement contained one or two inaccuracies of detail, but in
substance it was correct. Accordingly the newspapers
which were responsible for the publication of the
report decided to stick to their guns. Mr. Sandys
decided to proceed with his question, and other
M.P.s also put down questions on the same subject.

During the following weeks hardly a day passed
without the Chancellor of the Exchequer being bom-
barded with questions on the surrender of the Czech

gold by the Bank for International Settlements and
on the London negotiations for the surrender of the
blocked Czech assets. Under severe cross-examina-
tion by M.P.s on both sides of the House the Chancellor of the Exchequer reluctantly admitted that,
after all, Mr. Lloyd George's story was not a mare's-
nest. Almost every day brought new confession,
contradicting previous denials. Mr. Chamberlain himself had to intervene in the debate and put the
blame on the Treasury for having supplied him with
the information that Mr. Lloyd George's story was
entirely unfounded. On the first day it was admitted
that negotiations were in fact being pursued in London,
but it was stated that His Majesty's Government
had no means of knowing whether the Czech gold
held in London in the name of the Bank for International Settlements had in fact been surrendered.
On the following day Lord Simon went a step further
and admitted that, after all, His Majesty's Government did know that the Czech gold was surrendered,
but insisted that it received this information quite
unofficially from a Continental source. He laid special
stress on the fact that the British Directors of the
Bank for International Settlements did not inform
the Treasury, thereby clearing them of the grave
suspicion that they had acted as if they considered
themselves British subjects in the first place and
Directors of the Bank for International Settlements
in the second place only.

The official admission of the surrender of the Czech
gold to Germany aroused a storm of indignation which
led to a full-dress debate in the House of Commons
on May 26, 1939. During the course of this debate
the Government was attacked from all sides, and the

Chief Government Whip's efforts to find members defending the Government's point of view were entirely unavailing. In the circumstances the Government considered it expedient to postpone the negotiations with Germany for the surrender of further Czech assets, and the German delegates departed from London empty-handed. Owing to the persistence with which the Czech gold scandal was pursued in Parliament and in the Press during the following two months, the Treasury did not dare to resume negotiations with Germany. The appeasers were forced on the defensive, and in face of the barrage of criticisms they hesitated to commit fresh acts of appeasement. Mr. Chamberlain's " mare's-nest " — which in practice proved to be a " hornets' nest " — thus saved some Czech assets from being surrendered to Germany, and resulted in a temporary setback for appeasement.

Throughout May, June and July the question of the surrender of the gold remained in the forefront. Week after week new details were disclosed and the Chancellor of the Exchequer was forced to admit the facts at the rate of one tablespoonful at a time. At the same time he adopted the line that since both the Bank of England and the Bank for International Settlements were outside the Government's control, the Treasury had no means of preventing the surrender of the gold, or even of obtaining information concerning its whereabouts from the British Directors. He persistently referred to the " so-called Czech gold " and to the transaction between " a London bank " and " a Swiss bank ", which incidentally infuriated the Swiss banks who considered the Bank for International Settlements to be anything but Swiss, and who were annoyed by Dr. Beyen's statement that under Swiss banking law and practice he was justified in surrendering the Czech gold.

At the beginning of the campaign the Chancellor of the Exchequer went so far as to say that he was not even in a position to insist upon obtaining information on the matter from the Bank of England. After a conversation with Mr. Montagu Norman on May 26, 1939, however, he changed his line of defence and on the next occasion when the matter was raised he stated that the Bank of England itself had no means of knowing whether any part of the Czech gold held in London by the Bank for International Settlements belonged to the Czecho-Slovak National Bank. In this connection it may be worth while mentioning that on or about May 26 the method of accountancy of gold deposits between the Bank for International Settlements and the Bank of England was changed. Until then the deposit of each Central Bank held in London in the name of the Bank for International Settlements was held in a separate dossier. From that time onward all these various gold deposits were pooled together in a single dossier.

Beyond doubt this was a very convenient arrangement for all the parties concerned. Mr. Norman was now in a position to tell Lord Simon, and Lord Simon was henceforth in a position to tell Parliament, that the Bank of England had no means of knowing whether the Czech gold surrendered to the Reichsbank was still held in London. Herr Hechler, the Assistant General Manager of the Bank for International Settlements, frankly admitted in conversation with Mr. Josef Malik, former Foreign General Manager of the Czecho-Slovak National Bank, at Basle in

August 1939, that the object of the change was to avoid having to satisfy irksome inquiries about the gold transfer.

In face of the unanimity with which the House of Commons disapproved of the surrender of the gold, Lord Simon reluctantly admitted that its surrender was a deplorable act. When Mr. Duncan Sandys asked him whether he would make it clear to the Governor and Directors of the Bank of England that unless British representatives exercised in future a greater sense of responsibility in the performance of their functions, there would be a growing and insistent demand for the withdrawal of their privileges, Lord Simon replied, " I think the many questions which have been put and answered in this House on the subject will go to show the view that is taken in the House on this matter ". In banking circles it was felt that by giving this reply the Chancellor of the Exchequer had " thrown the Governor to the wolves ".

Nevertheless the surrender of the Czech gold was repeated on a smaller scale towards the end of August, a few days before the outbreak of the war. At the time of the surrender of the original £6 million of Czech gold the Reichsbank agreed to leave in London for the time being a deposit of over £1 million kept there for some special purpose by the Czecho-Slovak National Bank in the name of the Bank for International Settlements. During the second half of August the German authorities, knowing that Hitler was determined to embark upon a war, took steps to obtain the transfer of this deposit from London to Amsterdam and Berne. There was an opportunity for the Government and the Bank of England to prove that they genuinely regretted the transfer of

K

the original larger gold deposit. Notwithstanding the pooling of the various gold deposits held in the name of the Bank for International Settlements, Sir Otto Niemeyer in his capacity as Chairman of that bank presumably had the means of knowing about it, and he would have been in a position to inform the Treasury. Instead instructions for the transfer of the gold were promptly complied with.

Fortunately about that time M. Malik succeeded in escaping from Czecho-Slovakia and paid a visit to Basle, where he registered a vigorous protest on behalf of his bank (which he still represented) against the surrender of the gold in March. He told Dr. Beyen that should the Czecho-Slovak National Bank ever recover its freedom of action it would never have any dealings with the Bank for International Settlements. Dr. Beyen's reply was that he had no means of knowing that the instructions had been given under duress and that had he known it he would have acted otherwise. Thereupon M. Malik, in his capacity of a member of the Executive of the National Bank, instructed the Bank for International Settlements to block the gold deposit which was just being transferred from London to Amsterdam and Berne, and also a small Czech gold deposit held in Switzerland. A few days later the Bank for International Settlements was notified by the Czecho-Slovak National Bank that M. Malik's right to sign on behalf of the bank was cancelled. It was, however, too late. By that time steps had been taken to block in Amsterdam and Berne gold deposits amounting to some £1,620,000. This gold at any rate was saved from the Nazis, thanks to the firm line taken by M. Malik.

It seems probable that, consciously or otherwise, the attitude of the British authorities in the matter of the Czech gold was inspired by their desire to pursue a policy of appeasement. After having taken firm action in the matter of the Czech assets under the influence of the popular indignation over the occupation of Prague, they were evidently anxious not to antagonise Berlin unduly by going out of their way to save this particular gold deposit from being surrendered by the Bank for International Settlements. Admittedly the amount of £6 million was comparatively moderate. Considering, however, that Germany's gold stock was at a low ebb it must have come as a welcome windfall and enabled her to make eleventh-hour purchases of metals and other essential materials abroad. Translated in terms of arms and munitions those £6 million must have destroyed much British life and property.

CHAPTER XI

THE £1,000,000,000 LOAN SCHEME

THE eclipse of financial appeasement through the Czech gold scandal was necessarily temporary. The indignation aroused by the disclosures of May and June concerning the surrender of the Czech gold gradually died down, and with it the interest taken in the subject in Parliament and in the Press also subsided. Although the opponents of appeasement pursued their campaign even in July, it was becoming in the nature of flogging a dead horse. Plans were made for a revival of interest in the subject through legal action against the Bank of England by one of the London shareholders of the Czecho-Slovak National Bank, but before the necessary arrangements could be completed the war broke out and brought matters to an end.

Meanwhile the supporters of financial appeasement were awaiting an opportunity for a renewal of the Düsseldorf negotiations. The Treasury on its part was awaiting an opportunity for coming to terms with the German Government concerning the regularisation of the status of the blocked Czech assets at the cost of releasing in favour of Germany a large proportion of them. It was partly in order to discuss this matter that Herr Wohltat, one of Germany's super-negotiators, paid a visit to London in July 1939. The declared purpose of his visit was to participate in the International Whaling Conference held in

London, but, considering that he interrupted very important commercial negotiations in Spain in order to come here, it was reasonably obvious that he was after even bigger fish than whales.

Indeed it soon became known that he had had several discussions with Sir Horace Wilson and Mr. Hudson. London was seething with rumours about the nature and scope of these discussions.

The July 22 issue of the *Daily Telegraph* contained a detailed story according to which Mr. Hudson submitted to Herr Wohltat a proposal of a loan amounting to £1000 million for the purpose of enabling Germany to convert her industries from war requirements to peace requirements. The offer was subject to a fundamental modification of Germany's foreign policy, an undertaking of partial disarmament under international control and the evacuation of Czecho-Slovakia.

It is easy to imagine the effect of this bombshell. At first it was widely believed that the figure of the proposed loan was a printer's error and there was one nought too many. Subsequently the amount of £1000 million was confirmed by Mr. Hudson himself. Evidently the offer surpassed by a long way any previous acts of financial appeasement or attempts at financial appeasement. The fantastic size of the amount itself conveyed the impression that Great Britain was offering Danegeld to Germany in return for keeping the peace. What everybody wanted to know was whether Mr. Hudson made this offer in his personal capacity or on behalf of the British Government. Both Mr. Hudson and other officially inspired quarters emphasised that the offer was made entirely in his personal capacity, but many people were

inclined to take these assurances with a grain of salt.
Nor were their doubts dispelled by the statement
made by Mr. Chamberlain in the House of Commons
on July 24. He declared that he saw no harm in
conversations such as were pursued by Mr. Hudson
with Herr Wohltat. The fact that Mr. Hudson
remained a member of the Government in spite of
the uproar created by the scheme and that Sir Horace
Wilson was also in contact with Herr Wohltat may
be regarded as a conclusive proof that Mr. Chamberlain
was aware of the nature of Mr. Hudson's proposal.
While the details of the scheme may have been
Mr. Hudson's own ideas, in substance they must have
represented the Government's policy.

The British Press was unanimous in condemning
most emphatically the scheme. Probably for the
first time in history the leading articles of the *Daily
Herald* and the *Daily Mail* expressed exactly the same
views. It was feared that Mr. Hudson's move might
weaken the peace front which was then in the course
of formation, and that in any case it would be inter-
preted in Berlin as a sign of weakness. Apologists
of Mr. Hudson's proposals maintained that since the
projected loan was conditional upon disarmament by
Germany and the evacuation of Czecho-Slovakia, it
could not be regarded as an act of appeasement. In
reality the conditions provided no safeguard whatso-
ever against acts of bad faith on the part of Germany.
Germany could have well afforded to evacuate Czecho-
Slovakia and to make a beginning with disarmament
in order to gain possession of the proceeds of the loan.
Once this was done there would have been nothing to
prevent her from reoccupying defenceless Czecho-
Slovakia and resuming rearmament on an even larger

scale with the aid of the borrowed money on some trumped-up excuse of menace to Germany's security.

Surprisingly enough the plan met with unanimous opposition in the German Press. The time-honoured Nazi slogans about interest slavery, the golden calf and control of international finance were resurrected for the purpose. Yet it would be paying Hitler an undeserved compliment to suppose that the reason for this opposition was that he did not wish to go back on his previously declared opposition to international loans. Judging by the change of front regarding the anti-Communist policy of the Nazi régime it would have been easy to change its attitude overnight also in the matter of international loans and accept Mr. Hudson's offer.

The hostile attitude of the German Press towards the £1000 million loan scheme may be explained by Hitler's determination definitely to attack Poland in September. This being so, it would have been entirely useless to embark upon negotiations about the international loan since it would have taken months before its first instalment would have become available. Had it been possible to obtain an advance on it between July and September, Hitler would undoubtedly have jumped at the offer without modifying his decision to make war in September. Since, however, there would have been no chance to complete even preliminary talks by September, he could afford to reject indignantly the idea of bargaining away Germany's right to conquest in return for financial concessions. In any case, judging by the attitude of the British Press, it was obvious that it would have been extremely difficult if not impossible for the Government to obtain Parliament's approval for any such scheme. In such circumstances it cost nothing to Germany to make the gesture of rejecting what she would never have obtained in any case. Within a few days of its announcement the £1000 million loan scheme came to an ignominious end. Herr Wohltat returned to Berlin empty-handed, as after the uproar caused by the Hudson scheme the Government did not dare to make any concessions in any other direction.

In spite of this experience, the Government did not give up hope of striking a bargain with Hitler through financial appeasement. It is understood that the idea of British assistance to Germany in connection with the devaluation of the reichsmark was tentatively put forward by the British Directors of the Bank for International Settlements in the course of conversations with Funk at Basle. Sir Otto Niemeyer is known to have expressed particularly strong views that unless Germany devalued her currency economic collapse was inevitable. Even if this had been so, it may well be asked whether it would have been to Britain's advantage to save the Nazi régime. Although in theory the British Directors of the Bank for International Settlements acted entirely in their personal capacity, by sheer coincidence they are understood to have stated a point of view which was strongly supported in influential quarters in Whitehall. In British Government circles the view was held that, provided Germany changed her foreign policy, she could rely upon British assistance in the form of a loan enabling her to devalue the reichsmark and thus to maintain confidence in that currency at its devalued level.

Beyond doubt, the task of converting Germany's

war industries into peace industries would have been gigantic. Germany had, however, all the means at her disposal for carrying out this task without any extraordinary foreign assistance. Her productive capacity for machinery, and especially for machine tools, was second to that of no country, except possibly of the United States, and she was quite capable of manufacturing internally all the equipment required for the great transformation. It is true she would have required fairly substantial quantities of imported raw materials and gigantic capital resources to finance the conversion of her industries. Since, however, those raw materials and financial resources had been available for rearmament, they would have been available for the conversion of her industries as soon as the arms race was brought to a halt. There was no need whatever for a huge foreign loan to enable Germany to spend more on constructive machinery and less on destructive war material.

Regarding the projected British assistance to enable Germany to devalue the reichsmark, it is difficult to see why the reichsmark should have required support at a lower level, considering that it had been possible to maintain it at its overvalued level. In any case it is doubtful whether Germany wished to devalue. Under her peculiar system of foreign trade it was very convenient for her to maintain an overvalued reichsmark rate for certain purposes. It enabled her to pay prices in excess of the world market prices for various products, and since she could only pay by means of exports her increased purchases abroad entailed a corresponding increase of her sales abroad. Admittedly, she had to subsidise her exports, but if her export trade had been stimulated through a devaluation of the reichsmark she would have had to subsidise her imports, so that from a budgetary point of view there was nothing to choose between the existing state of affairs and the one that would have been created by devaluation.

Nor was it strictly correct to say that the reichsmark was overvalued. While the official rate was maintained at its overvalued parity, there were many different kinds of subsidiary reichsmark rates which were depreciated to a considerable degree. This elastic system suited Germany's purpose, and it is difficult to see what great advantages she would have gained by replacing it with the more rigid orthodox system.

Evidently Germany did not need any foreign loan, either for the purpose of converting her war industries into peace industries — if indeed she intended to do so — or for the purpose of devaluing the reichsmark — if indeed she intended to do so. This does not mean that she did not require a foreign loan at all. Had it not been for the fact that Hitler was determined to attack Poland in September, long before any part of the loan would have become available, he would undoubtedly have seized upon an offer which would have enabled Germany to build up a powerful gold and foreign exchange reserve — for war purposes. In order to replenish his war chest he would have been only too pleased to accept support from the despised international financiers. Since, however, he could not have his cake and eat it, he preferred to start his war without waiting for a foreign loan.

The whole idea that war could be averted by means of financial or economic concessions to Germany was based on the false assumption that the main cause for Hitler's aggressive attitude lay in Germany's intolerable economic position. There could be nothing further from the truth. To give the devil his due, it must be admitted that under the Nazi régime Germany succeeded in increasing her production to a truly remarkable degree. Had it not been for Hitler's determination to rearm, such expansion of production would have resulted in an unprecedented improvement in the standard of living in Germany. Had Hitler and Goering not preferred guns to butter, the milliards spent on rearmament could have been spent on the improvement of housing conditions and the increase of consumption goods available for the population. This would have been possible with the aid of the planned economy and expansionary monetary system introduced by the Nazi régime without thereby affecting the country's capacity to export and import. Germany could easily have become one of the most prosperous countries even in the complete absence of any special financial or economic concessions by Great Britain for the purpose of appeasement.

Hitler was determined to conquer Europe and no economic or financial concession could possibly have altered his determination. Had it been possible to carry through the Düsseldorf deal or the Hudson scheme, the only result would have been to enable Germany to buy up gigantic stocks of oil and other raw materials before embarking upon the inevitable war of aggression.

CHAPTER XII·

THE outbreak of the war in September 1939 clearly proved the utter failure of the policy of appeasement. One would have thought that since the futility of that policy became so glaringly evident the appeasers would realise their mistake and the spirit of appeasement would give way to a spirit of stern determination to fight the war to a victorious conclusion. Instead, the spirit of appeasement continued to prevail to a considerable degree even after the outbreak of the war. While in official quarters it confined itself to a weak and lenient attitude towards non-belligerents and neutrals, among unofficial appeasers the idea of appeasing Germany continued to reign supreme, war or no war.

During the early part of the war Italy was the chief beneficiary of this policy of appeasement. It was the natural continuation of the policy that was responsible for the conclusion of the Mediterranean Pact between Mr. Chamberlain and Signor Mussolini following upon the liquidation of the sanctions. Before the ink was dry on this pact it was already violated by Mussolini, who thus beat even Hitler's speed record in dishonouring newly given pledges. Even before this stillborn pact was concluded there was much evidence of appeasement in relation to Italy. As a result the sanctions became reduced to a farce. They were not applied to oil imports, even though from the point of view of Italy's ability to defy the League oil was more important than all the other imports added together. It was feared that should sanctions be extended to include oil Italy might be driven to embarking upon a war against Great Britain before her oil supplies were exhausted. In order to appease her she was allowed to replenish those supplies, which of course reduced to absurdity the whole system of sanctions.

Evidently we got the worst of both worlds. There might have been something to be said in favour of a realistic policy by which the League would have confined opposition to the conquest of Abyssinia to formal protest, as in the case of the Japanese conquest of Manchukuo, in order to maintain the Stresa Front against Germany. The alternative would have been to enforce sanctions rigidly at the risk of a war in the Mediterranean. But to antagonise Italy by the application of ineffective sanctions without being prepared to carry those sanctions far enough to make them effective was the height of absurdity.

After the liquidation of the sanctions efforts were made to conciliate Italy. These efforts assumed partly the form of financial appeasement. Italy was granted very favourable terms for the liquidation of her pre-sanction debts and she was treated with great consideration in her trade negotiations with this country. At the same time the banks were given to understand that the Government was no longer against resuming the granting of credits to Italy on their own responsibility. While during the sanctions the banking credits were liquidated, during 1937–1938 a large proportion of these credits was reopened once more, though in many cases the lending banks insisted upon adequate security. During that period London was literally swarming with Italian loan proposals. The Italian Government itself refrained from applying to the City for loans but private negotiators were working overtime. They ranked from the duly authorised negotiators of standing to self-appointed agents. Whenever the activities of the latter were reported in the Press the Italian authorities indignantly repudiated the suggestion that they were in the market for a loan. Nevertheless, had these shady intermediaries succeeded in concluding a deal, their official status would immediately have been recognised. Fortunately by that time bankers became very cautious. Italian " non-intervention " in Spain carried the possibility of international complications, and in such circumstances it would have been grossly imprudent to issue a loan for Italy. Efforts aiming at the adoption of a policy of financial appeasement of Italy before the war failed completely.

The idea of appeasing Italy with the aid of a loan gained new strength after the outbreak of the war. In many quarters it was believed that it would be possible to bribe Mussolini into remaining neutral by granting Italy a very large loan. While the amounts negotiated before the war were small, the figures mentioned after the outbreak of the war were very substantial. The amount of £75 million was one of the popular rumours. Evidently Italy's price had gone up. These rumours never received confirmation and Mussolini had no opportunity for repeating the experience with the Mediterranean Pact by cashing the loan and then joining his partner of the Axis. There can be no doubt that the granting of such a loan, together with the granting of various political concessions, would have made no difference to Italy's determination to enter the war when it appeared as if Germany was winning it. Had the appeasers succeeded in persuading the Government to grant such a loan, it would only have enabled Italy to build up vast raw material reserves during her period of non-belligerency.

As it was she was given every opportunity to build up such reserves within the limits of her none-too-plentiful foreign exchange resources. Even at the time when Italy's entry into the war was evidently a matter of weeks she was allowed to import unlimited quantities of oil and other vital war materials. Indeed during the period of non-belligerency Italy increased her oil imports to a very considerable extent. Rumanian and Russian oil was pouring in through Trieste and American and Mexican oil through Genoa. Italy stocked herself with oil to the limit of her storage capacity.

What is worse, a very considerable part of Italy's imports of oil and other raw materials found its way to Germany. During the first eight months of the war Italy provided easily the most important gap through which the blockade was evaded. The British authorities were anxious not to antagonise her and to treat her imports in a spirit of understanding and appeasement. It is true, representatives of the Ministry of Economic Warfare were appointed to keep a watchful eye on the chief Italian ports, but notwithstanding this goods were pouring through Italy to and from Germany. Genoa and Trieste experienced an almost unprecedented wave of prosperity as a result of this transit traffic.

Whenever the question of blockade evasion through Italy was raised in Parliament during the early months of the war the then Minister of Economic Warfare, Mr Ronald Cross, went out of his way to deny or minimise the leakage. Subsequently, however, after Italy's entry into the war it was freely admitted in official quarters that during her period of non-belligerency Italy had rendered extremely valuable services to Germany by helping her to evade the blockade.

When in November 1939 the blockade was extended over German exports an exemption was granted in favour of German coal shipments to Italy. Negotiations were pursued to come to an agreement by which to replace these shipments by British coal shipments, and one of the proposals which the Government was inclined to accept was that payment should be made largely in the form of Italian vegetables. Considering that France was still in a position to cover the British requirements — which, thanks to the success of the "Dig for Victory" campaign, were declining in any case — the proposed solution was far from ideal. Negotiations were dragging on month after month and meanwhile Italy was allowed to continue to import by sea millions of tons of German coal. It was not until the end of February that this form of appeasement was brought to an end. Even then several Italian ships carrying German coal from Rotterdam, which were seized by the British contraband control, were released on the understanding that in future this traffic must stop.

There is no reason whatever to suppose that the attempt at appeasing Italy by means of such leniency postponed her intervention in the war by a single day. The reason why Italy did not join Germany before June 1940 was that she was sitting on the fence. Even if the blockade had been enforced strictly she would not have risked a war while the French Army was still intact. And even if appeasement had been carried much further she would have seized the opportunity of stabbing France in the back after her resistance had been crushed by Germany.

What is true concerning Italy is also true concerning the third partner in the Tripartite Pact. The Order in Council extending the blockade over German exports was not enforced very strictly regarding German exports to Japan. A large order for synthetic oil plant was placed in Germany by Japan some time before the war and the machinery and equipments were being delivered by the sea route. Several substantial consignments were allowed to proceed to their destination after the embargo on German exports was supposed to have become effective. Admittedly, this machinery could have been sent by rail, and there is good reason to suppose that in more recent months it was sent by that route. The same is true concerning German coal exports to Italy. One of the advantages of stopping German sea-borne exports was exactly that it increased the pressure upon the limited facilities of the overburdened German railway system.

Another way in which Japan was hoped to be appeased during the early months of the war was through the purchase of Japanese goods of second-rate importance by Great Britain and the British Empire. It is difficult to justify the expenditure of foreign exchange on cheap toys, Christmas crackers and Japanese silk stockings in time of war when the requirements of war materials and essential food imports were depleting the foreign exchange reserve.

L

Diplomatic considerations were allowed, however, to prevail.

After the invasion of Holland the Dutch East Indies came under Allied control. It would have been possible, in view of Japan's openly hostile attitude towards the Allies, to stop Japanese oil imports from the Dutch East Indies. The same considerations, however, which were responsible for the closing of the Burma Road induced the Allies to abstain from depriving Japan from rather more than her normal share in the oil production of the Dutch East Indies. In a true spirit of appeasement she was allowed to increase her imports. Nor were the American oil companies prevailed upon by the United States Government to abstain from supplying a potential enemy with the means which may enable him to strike at the British Empire and at the United States. Even though an embargo was placed on the export of certain kinds of high-grade oil, this did not effectively prevent Japan from obtaining American aviation petrol.

The same diplomatic considerations which were responsible for the policy of appeasement pursued in relation to Italy and Japan did not apply to the smaller neutral countries in Europe. There was no reason to worry about the possibility of Holland, Belgium or the Scandinavian countries joining Germany in a war against the democracies. Nevertheless, even in relation to them a policy of appeasement was applied. They too were allowed to import contraband goods far in excess of their requirements, even though it was evident that a large percentage of the surplus found its way to Germany. Conceivably this attitude was inspired by a desire to appease not the countries concerned but Germany, by making it worth her while to abstain from violating their neutrality. In reality in this instance, as in every other instance, the policy of appeasement produced the opposite effect to what it was meant to produce. As the small neutral countries of Northern and Western Europe were allowed to build up large raw-material stocks, the inducement for Germany to invade them became stronger. After the conquest of the Low Countries Germany secured in these countries huge quantities of essential supplies which strengthened her raw-material position to no slight extent.

The Government's attitude towards neutral countries in South-Eastern Europe also flavoured of appeasement. No adequate pressure was brought to bear upon either Hungary or Rumania or Bulgaria to induce them to refuse to become tools of the Axis. In the case of Hungary the attitude of the Foreign Office in face of her impending decision to sign the Axis Pact was one of sweet reasonableness. Hungarian official circles themselves were amazed at the complete lack of pressure upon her on the part of Great Britain. When following upon the signing of the pact the Hungarian Minister paid a visit to the Foreign Office in order to explain his Government's attitude, he fully expected to hear hard words. Instead he was told that H.M. Government quite understood the difficulties of Hungary's position and that they were fully aware that she could not have acted otherwise. When it was an open secret that German troop trains were passing through Hungary to Rumania, the Government abstained from taking action. Yet firm action at that stage might have modified considerably subsequent developments in the Balkans. There was every justification for bombing the Hungarian State Railways in order to delay the unresisted German invasion of Rumania. Considering that in any case the Hungarian railway system was overburdened by the transport of goods consignments for Germany from the Balkans, its disorganisation through air attacks against railway bridges and junctions might have increased Germany's difficulties to no slight extent. What is more important, it might have stiffened the attitude of Rumania and Bulgaria. As it was, no attempt was made to offset German pressure upon them by British pressure in the opposite direction. Threats of aerial bombardment of their lines of communication and vital industries, together with threats that their attitude would be remembered at the peace conference, might have induced these countries to adopt a firmer attitude in face of the German penetration. The only step taken against these countries was to withhold Navicerts from them when it became obvious that they would join the Axis.

One of the outstanding mistakes of this war was the failure of the British Government to bomb the Rumanian oil refineries and storage tanks the moment Rumania admitted German troops to her territory. For some inscrutable reason the British diplomatic representative was allowed to remain in Bucharest to watch helplessly the growth of German military penetration and to reassure with his presence the Rumanian Government that no such action was contemplated. The quantity of oil Germany can receive from Rumania is one of the major factors which will determine the outcome and duration of this war. It

would have been of the utmost importance, therefore,
to find means for reducing Rumania's capacity to
supply Germany with oil. Admittedly, the task of
bombing the oilfields themselves is by no means easy.
The targets are too widely separated and require
systematic bombing which may have been beyond
the capacity of the Royal Air Force. On the other
hand, it would have been easy to bomb the refineries,
and in doing so the refining capacity at Germany's
disposal would have become materially reduced. One
of the favourite arguments against the bombing of
the Rumanian oilfields was that it was easier to reach
the Rumanian oil after its arrival in Germany than
while still in Rumania. As a matter of fact, while
Rumanian crude oil imports have to be refined in
German refineries, Rumanian refined products can be
sent straight to their final destination and are therefore dispersed. Another argument against the bombing of Rumanian oil was that owing to transport
difficulties it would be impossible in any case for
Germany to increase materially her imports of oil
from Rumania. Subsequent events have proved that
this problem was also capable of solution. Instead
of sending Rumanian oil to the German Army the
German Army was sent to the Rumanian oil. A very
large part of the Rumanian output which could not at
the time be transported to Germany could be transported to the German troops in the Balkans. The
simplification of the problem of oil supply must have
facilitated the task of conquering Yugoslavia and
Greece. After the conquest of the latter it became
possible for Germany to use the sea route for the
transport of oil, so that this problem became practically
solved.

Appeasers who were opposed to pressure upon the countries of South-Eastern Europe relied upon legalistic and sentimental arguments to make out a case in favour of their policy. It was argued with very little convincing force that since Hungary, Rumania and Bulgaria were technically neutral even though they admitted German technicians and tourists, it would be an act of aggression to bomb them. It was also argued that it is hardly fair to press a small country to resist Germany, especially so long as Great Britain is not in a position to render them very effective assistance. The arguments put forward by the diplomats of the small countries that they were in any case unable to resist the weight of a German attack for more than a few days was cheerfully accepted by appeasers in this country. Thanks to their attitude, it has come to be assumed that it is Great Britain's job to fight the battle of small countries even if the latter abstained from assisting her in that task. Yet there is a perfect answer to the argument that resistance by any one of the small countries would make no difference. Every little helps, and if resistance by a small country means that Germany has to use up so many hundreds of thousands of tons of petrol and other war materials, tanks, planes and human material, then the small country concerned has done her bit, even though her resistance was crushed. The cost for Germany of overcoming the resistance of half a dozen small countries may make an appreciable difference to the outcome and duration of the war.

Notwithstanding this, British policy always aimed at abstaining from unduly pressing small countries to resist. German propaganda invented a most ingenious formula by which even the very feeble and half-hearted diplomatic efforts of Great Britain to stiffen the attitude of small countries in face of German penetration was denounced as a sinister attempt to expand the scope of the war. Yet it is fairly obvious that in no case were the small countries pressed to commit acts of aggression against Germany. In every case it was they who were invaded and it was Germany who expanded the scope of the war. In any case, considering that Germany constitutes a menace to the freedom of the world, there would be every justification for inducing countries which have so far escaped her domination to take the initiative for self-defence instead of meekly awaiting their turn to be slaughtered. There would be nothing to be ashamed for if British diplomacy could initiate and organise a world-wide crusade against the Axis.

It is high time to discard this feeble policy of appeasement in relation to neutral countries. There is no place for any misplaced sentimentalism in the conduct of British foreign policy. In the olden days Great Britain could afford to be sentimental. In present circumstances, however, with her very existence at stake, she must pursue a very firm and completely realistic foreign policy.

CHAPTER XIII

APPEASEMENT OF GERMANY DURING THE WAR

THE outbreak of the war did not bring to an end the activities of those who before the war had sought to appease Germany. Some of them considered it wise to efface themselves for a time in the hope that their pre-war activities would be forgiven and forgotten. The bolder amongst them, however, continued their good work though with different methods.

Admittedly, the numerical strength of the camp of unrepentant appeasers is at the time of writing negligible. The predominant majority of the British nation, under Mr. Churchill's inspiring leadership, is firmly determined to fight this war to a victorious conclusion. Nevertheless, it would be a mistake to ignore the attitude of the minority which might be able, in given circumstances, to increase its influence over the public.

Among the various groups of appeasers the British Fascists remained very active until their newspaper was suppressed and their leaders were arrested under the Defence Regulations. Other pre-war appeasers considered it advisable, however, to keep very quiet. They were allowed to fade into the background, for " No recriminations for the past " was the popular slogan. The City ceased to be a stronghold of appeasement. Most of the bankers who before the war distinguished themselves in that sphere either realised their mistake or decided that since their country was

now at war with Germany there was no choice for them
but to do their share in the general war effort. It
is true pro-German sympathy was not dead. In
1939 a committee was formed for the purpose of
collecting funds in order to help German internees and
prisoners of war. The chairman of that committee
was Mr. Helmuth Schroeder and the bankers were
the banking house J. Henry Schroeder & Co. The
matter was raised in the House of Commons and
Mr. Oliver Stanley, the then Secretary of State for
War, declared emphatically his disapproval of the
activities of the committee, on the ground that
German prisoners of war are well provided with
what they need and there was no need for supple-
menting it by means of private collection. Most
people in the City and in Parliament were amazed by
the strange attitude displayed by the Schroeder family.

Curiously enough, a number of pre-war appeasers
managed to find jobs for themselves in the Ministry
of Economic Warfare. While their loyalty was above
suspicion, it is permissible to doubt whether their
pre-war error of judgment specially qualified them
for their jobs.

There was a remarkable proportion of appeasers
among various classes of currency reformers. The
Duke of Bedford is one of the outstanding examples.
Presumably the fanatics of various schools of monetary
reform have a sneaking admiration for Hitler and the
Nazi system on account of its disregard of orthodox
monetary considerations.

The policy of appeasement advocated by the
various schools has assumed a totally different form
since the war. There is no longer any question of
openly suggesting that Germany's claims should be

satisfied. For one thing Germany has helped herself to territories the surrender of which before the war might have been the aim of the appeasement policy. Most appeasers do not even go so far as to advocate that Germany should be left in undisturbed possession of her conquests and that peace should be concluded on that basis. Apart from Mr. Maxton and a few other left-wing politicians, nobody dares to advocate openly the initiation of negotiations of peace with Hitler. They prefer to remain pleasantly vague on the subject whether the existence of a Nazi régime in Germany should be regarded as an insurmountable obstacle to peace negotiations. What is more, while they constantly urge the Government to state its precise peace aims, they themselves carefully avoid committing themselves to any statement about the extent of concessions which should be offered to Hitler in order to induce him to conclude peace.

The extreme wing of appeasers is represented by a group of neo-isolationsists who believe that so long as Great Britain is able to maintain her control of the seas it would not matter if Hitler were to be left in control of the entire Continent, including the channel ports. This doctrine was expounded in a book entitled *Sea Power*, written by a well-known author on naval subjects under the pseudonym of " T. 124 ". What these neo-isolationists fail to realise is that if Germany were to be left in direct or indirect control of the shipyards and iron ore resources of continental countries she would easily outbuild Great Britain in a race for naval supremacy. The experience of the *Bismarck* has shown that the quality of both German warships and German crews is first-class. Should Germany succeed in building a fleet larger than the Royal Navy — which in any case is handicapped by its world-wide commitments — this country might lose control of the seas and would be at the mercy of the superior German land forces.

A much more dangerous campaign of appeasement is the one initiated by Commander Stephen King-Hall, M.P. He advocates a compromise which would leave Germany strong and powerful. To make his scheme palatable he declares that his aim is " total victory " (even though what he has in mind is not total and it is not victory) as distinct from a mere military victory. His argument runs broadly on the following lines :—In order to achieve what he calls " total victory " (that is, a treaty that secures lasting peace) it is not necessary for this country to win military victory. In support of this contention he quotes historical examples to prove that in the past military victories did not secure lasting peace, and that, conversely, on occasions lasting peace was secured even in the absence of military victory. It would be easy, however, to marshal a much more impressive array of historical examples in refutation of Commander King-Hall's thesis.

Commander King-Hall's campaign is of such a nature as to inspire pessimism regarding the possibilities of inflicting defeat on Germany, whether through military or economic weapons. He seeks to minimise the extent to which even in case of supremacy in the air the R.A.F. would be capable of destroying Germany's economic war potential. To characterise his methods of argument, let it be sufficient to quote his remark in Chapter VII of his book, saying that since the average distance from British aerodromes to German targets is three times that between German

controlled aerodromes and British targets, three times
as many British bombers would be required to inflict
the same amount of damage on Germany as Germany
is capable of inflicting on this country. This seems
to be based on the assumption that German bombers
were in the habit of making three trips over England
during one night. Even then, Commander King-
Hall's arithmetic failed to allow for the difficulties
and loss of time involved in taking off and landing.
He argues at some length why it is hopeless to try
to disorganise the enemy's transport system, but
beyond a casual reference he does not deal with the
question of paralysing Germany by destroying her
oil plants and oil supplies. In the following chapter
on " Economic Warfare " he continues to ignore
Germany's Achilles heel — the vulnerability of her oil
supply. He tries to prove that amidst existing conditions it is hopeless to expect the blockade to paralyse
Germany economically. His conclusion is that the
blockade cannot in the present circumstances amount
to more than a considerable nuisance to Germany.
The word " oil " is not even mentioned in this
chapter. Beyond doubt, the admission of the effec-
tiveness of the blockade regarding oil would materially
weaken Commander King-Hall's thesis. But he is
determined to prove that there is very little to hope
from the blockade and, therefore, a German oil problem simply does not exist for him.

Should Commander King-Hall succeed in inducing
the British public to accept his views that it is
both superfluous and impossible to defeat Germany
by means of military victory and economic warfare,
the effect would be that the nation's determination to
fight this war to a victorious conclusion would become

undermined. The mind of the British public would then become receptive to suggestions of a peace of compromise. In all fairness to Commander King-Hall, it is necessary to admit that he emphatically repudiates the idea of concluding peace with Hitler and the present régime in Germany. What he wants is a sweeping political offensive to try to induce the German people to repudiate its present leaders. To that end he would like this country to advocate peace terms which would appear acceptable to the German people. He would like the Government to commit itself to promises with the aid of which he hopes to persuade the Germans that it is to their interest to overthrow Hitler and make peace. It is in order to make out a case in favour of promising such concessions to Germany that he paints the prospects of a military victory with such gloomy colours. Yet it is simply past comprehension that anyone should imagine for a moment that even the most sweeping promises and the most skilful propaganda could possibly induce the German people to revolt against the Nazi régime unless and until the German Armed Forces are defeated, or, at any rate, until the German people realise the imminence of such a defeat.

The majority of those who agitate in favour of declaring the Government's peace aims are fully aware that such peace aims as they have in mind would be entirely unacceptable to Hitler. What they have in mind is that the Government should make a binding declaration promising to let Germany off lightly after the British victory. They accept the German propaganda argument that the Versailles Treaty was wicked and cruel, and maintain that since the method of firmness failed a conciliatory policy

should be given a chance. Most of those who advocate this course can be divided into two classes, the
right-wing pro-Germans and their left-wing dupes.
The policy of adopting towards Germany an attitude
of " heads you win, tails you won't lose " is the logical
continuation of the pro-German policy of appeasement before the war. This policy is powerfully
supported by a large number of left-wing politicians
who are entirely oblivious of the fact that they play
the game of Ribbentrop's friends. They imagine that
in opposing firm measures to prevent Germany from
repeating her acts of aggression of 1914 and 1939
they serve the interests of the German Socialists, who,
they feel, should not be made to pay the penalty for
the wickedness of their brothers the German Nazis.
What they overlook is that after the advent of Hitler
the millions of German Communists and Socialists
joined the ranks of the Nazis with very few exceptions,
and since then they have given Hitler their whole-
hearted support. The fact is that the reactionary
Junkers and big industrialists in Germany are at
present practically the only anti-Nazis left. Needless to say, they are in no way less aggressive and
Imperialistic than the Nazis themselves and they
support Hitler because he satisfies their Imperialistic
ambitions.

One of the methods applied by the appeasers is
to disarm any hatred of the Germans that tends to
develop among the British public. They fear that
should the wave of hatred be allowed to proceed
public opinion would press the Government at the
moment of victory to insist upon harsh peace terms.
In order to avoid the recurrence of the experience of
1918–1919 they are doing their utmost to induce the

British public to forgive their German foes even
before they are defeated. They themselves are prepared to forgive not only the atrocities committed
by the Germans but also those which they will commit
in the future. Further indiscriminate bombing of
civilian populations, the use of poison gas and other
acts violating the rules of international law and those
of human decency are forgiven in advance for the
sake of preventing the development of a strong wave
of hatred which might otherwise interfere with their
plans of letting Germany off lightly after her defeat.

Those in favour of appeasement have acquired the
habit of referring to Germans as " Nazis ". They
talk about the " Nazi army ", the " Nazi air force ",
etc., merely in order to convey the impression that
any atrocities committed by Germans are in reality
committed by them in their capacity of Nazis and
that the German people as a whole, as distinct from
the Nazi régime, should not be held responsible for
them. At the beginning of the war official British
propaganda was inclined to follow this line, but
fortunately it was abandoned after the Government
realised the extent to which the German nation
identifies itself with its Nazi rulers. On the other
hand, the various schools of appeasers continue to
apply this entirely unjustified and grossly misleading
discrimination between Germans and Nazis.

Left-wing appeasers admittedly act in perfect good
faith even though they pursue a short-sighted policy.
Right-wing appeasers, on the other hand, exploit the
misplaced humanitarian feelings of their left-wing
dupes for the purpose of preparing a peace of compromise with Hitler. The first step in that direction
is to influence British public opinion in favour of

generous peace terms to Germany after British victory. Once their point of view is widely accepted it would become much easier to induce the British public to accept a peace of compromise with the present German régime. A stage may be reached when the difference between the terms advocated by the appeasers and those demanded by Hitler will become, on paper at any rate, negligible. Once this stage is reached, then the next move will be to persuade British public opinion that in the circumstances it is hardly worth while to continue the war merely because of our dislike of Germany's internal régime. It will then be argued that, after all, it is for the German nation to choose its régime and its leader, and that it would be contrary to the principles of democracy for this country to wage war against the German nation merely because of our disapproval of the Nazi régime or of Hitler. They will, of course, never admit the fact that peace with Hitler on any terms would be merely an armistice providing him with an opportunity to replenish his supplies of essential raw materials.

At the present stage in the programme of appeasement the British public is sought to be persuaded that the Germans are really kind and decent people and that it is only the Nazis who are wicked. At the next stage in the programme efforts will be made to reassure the British people that, after all, even the Nazis are not necessarily wicked, and that there is a good deal to be said in favour of that régime. This is in fact already being done to a considerable extent. In a book entitled *The Social Policy of Nazi Germany*, Mr. C. W. Guillebaud presents in glowing colours the picture of the achievements of the Nazi régime in

Germany in the social sphere. He pays little attention to the glaring discrepancies between the Nazi
achievements on paper and in practice, and emphatically endorses the view that there is general content-
ment among the working classes. He represents that
advanced school of appeasers who maintain that not
only the Germans but even the Nazis are on the
whole a decent lot. Though he takes care to point
out that he disapproves of the Gestapo and concentration camps, in the same breath he states that
" fortunately [*sic*] for human happiness it is possible
to get accustomed even to the perpetual dark shadow
of the Gestapo and concentration camps, and it may
be doubted whether the average German worker is as
acutely conscious of it in his daily life as the foreign
observer is apt to imagine ". Presumably sooner or
later we shall come across an even more advanced
school of appeasers who will out-Guillebaud Mr.
Guillebaud by arguing with great convincing force
that, after all, even the Gestapo is on the whole a
decent institution! All this helps to prepare the
ground for a peace of compromise with Hitler.
Similarly the effort to whitewash Hitler's scheme for
a " New Order in Europe " prepares the ground for
proposals allowing Germany to retain at least economic control over certain parts of Europe, and
possibly even political control. About this more will
be said in the next chapter.

The unwisdom of the method of disarming hatred
against the undefeated foe while this country is
fighting for its very existence cannot be sufficiently
emphasised. At a time when the outcome of the
war depends upon the intensity of the nation's
economic war effort it is a suicidal course to weaken

M

that war effort for the sake of appeasement. It is a well-known fact that hate is a very strong incentive for an intensification of the economic war effort. It is argued sometimes that the British nation can fight this war to a successful finish even without hating its opponent, simply as a result of the realisation that its very existence is threatened and that it is fighting, not because it hates the Germans, but in defence of its freedom and existence. Unfortunately the real extent of the danger of being enslaved in case of German victory is even now not adequately realised. Many people continue to think of this war in terms of previous wars when defeat only meant unfavourable peace terms and nothing more. It is still considered inconceivable that the British island fortress should ever be conquered. This being so, the necessity of putting every ounce of our energy into our war effort is not generally realised. Nothing short of the initial success of an attempt at invasion would bring home to the great masses the extent and imminence of their danger. In the absence of that powerful incentive — and obviously it would be preferable if it remained absent — we have to depend for an intensification of the economic war effort largely upon the hatred of the enemy. Experience has proved that after some particularly outrageous atrocity of the *Luftwaffe* the output in the region affected shows a distinct improvement, because the workmen, enraged by the sight of destruction caused in their own immediate neighbourhood, want to hit back and can only do so by intensifying their work. In the circumstances it is foolish in the extreme to seek to demobilise hatred for the sake of securing conciliatory peace terms to Germany after a British victory.

That victory is still a long way ahead and it can
only be achieved with the aid of the maximum of
war effort. And if the appeasers succeed in weakening
the war effort, then this country may not be in a position to fix the peace terms, conciliatory or otherwise.

What is equally important is the effect of the ill-
advised efforts of the appeasers to disarm hate upon
the population of conquered countries. In any case
there is a widespread conception on the Continent
that Great Britain forgives too easily in the hour of
victory. Suffering intensely under the German domination, the conquered peoples resent the idea of such
generosity, since they feel that it will be largely at
their expense. Being Germany's immediate neigh-
bours, they feel they know the Germans much better
than most British people can possibly know them,
and they are utterly convinced that the only way to
prevent Germany from invading them once more
would be by depriving her of the means to do so.
From the point of view of the present argument it
is entirely immaterial whether they are right or wrong
in this assumption. What matters is that they feel
very strongly about it and that they are emphatically
in favour of a stern peace. What they fear is that
after a British victory Germany will be left united
and strong, while Great Britain, in accordance with
her traditions, will disarm. It is argued that after
the last war it took the British nation twenty years
to overcome its war-weariness and to be prepared
once more to stand up to German aggression, while
Germany recovered from her war-weariness much
sooner. It is also pointed out that while it took
Germany twenty years to recover her pre-1914
military power, which was destroyed by Versailles,

in case of a conciliatory peace she would be in a much better position to recover her pre-war strength in a much shorter time. And since Great Britain would still be war-weary at a time when Germany would be ready to act once more, the chances are that she would meet with even less opposition than during the present war in her effort to regain control over the European continent.

On the basis of these views it might seem tempting to conclude that it is not worth while for the oppressed peoples to risk their lives by resisting the oppressor if even in case of victory their freedom would at best only be restored temporarily. Rather than expose themselves to the consequences of resistance to Germany, to the additional destruction which will accompany their liberation and a few years later to the additional destruction through a fresh German invasion, they may prefer to resign themselves to their present fate and make the best of a bad job by collaborating with their oppressors. The logical outcome of appeasement in Great Britain is a decline in the active and passive resistance to German domination on the Continent. The extent to which this would affect the chances of victory could hardly be exaggerated. Admittedly, appeasement is only preached in unofficial British quarters, but since the appeasement school is very vocal while their opponents are, on the whole, reluctant to run into print, a wide-spread impression may develop that the majority of the British nation is in favour of appeasement. Should the appeasers succeed in persuading the Government to endorse their views, the result upon the attitude of the oppressed nations would be fatal. Should, on the other hand, the Government, at the

risk of the disapproval of a small but vocal minority,
repudiate emphatically the policy of appeasement, it
would inevitably produce a very salutary effect upon
the attitude of the conquered peoples. There is every
reason to believe that the Government, especially
Mr. Churchill himself, is strongly against " soft "
peace terms, but in the interest of national unity
is reluctant to open such a controversial issue at
the present stage. This being so, Lord Vansittart's
personal intervention in the controversy was highly
salutary. Although he broadcast his strong anti-
appeasement views in his personal capacity, nevertheless, since he was the Chief Diplomatic Adviser to
the Government, his personal views were bound to
make a profound impression. In so far as they came
to the notice of the conquered peoples they must
have derived much comfort from the evidence that
one of the leading officials of the British Government was allowed to express even in his personal
capacity such pronounced views against the policy
of appeasement.

It goes without saying that Lord Vansittart's
broadcast and its subsequent reproduction in
pamphlet form created consternation in the camp of
appeasement. It also provided an opportunity for
appeasers who since the war have remained silent
to come out into the open. In the House of Lords
Lord Vansittart was attacked by appeasers such
as Lord Londonderry, Lord Ponsonby and Lord
Arnold. In the House of Commons Lady Astor and
Mr. Richard Stokes sought in vain to induce the
Government to repudiate its Chief Diplomatic Adviser.
The Times attacked him in a leading article, though
for considerations of expediency the attack assumed

the form of objection to the alleged precedent created by Lord Vansittart in taking part in a political controversy in spite of his status as a Government official. *The Times* chose to ignore the fact that the publication of political views by a civil servant with the permission of the political head of his department has long been a recognised practice.

It was only to be expected that the appeasers would react vigorously to Lord Vansittart's broadcast, and it took the moral courage of Lord Vansittart to face such an onslaught. The great majority of people who share his views prefer to keep them to themselves. They have been effectively terrorised into silence by the militant appeasers. The situation is somewhat similar to the one that existed some six years ago when the necessity for rearmament was becoming increasingly evident, but when, in spite of this, anyone who dared to put forward suggestions to that effect was the subject of attack and abuse on the part of appeasers. It required considerable moral courage to face accusations of being a warmonger and veiled allusions of being in the pay of arms manufacturers. Most people, including leading members of the Government, lacked that moral courage, and that is the reason why the war found this country so badly prepared. Similarly most people who realise the necessity for depriving Germany of the opportunity of repeating her aggression lack the moral courage to say so for fear of being denounced as reactionary Imperialists and warmongers. Unless and until a large number of politicians and journalists are prepared to face such accusations, it will be difficult to counteract the mischievous effects of appeasement propaganda.

CHAPTER XIV

ECONOMIC RUNCIMANISM

In 1938 the turning-point in the Czech-Slovak crisis was provided by the publication of one of the conclusions arrived at by Lord Runciman on his return from his investigation of the Sudeten German problem. He stated that even if the Allies were to win the war against Germany it would be necessary to comply with the universal desire of the Sudeten Germans to be joined to the Reich. This conclusion was largely responsible for disarming the determination of Great Britain to stand by Czecho-Slovakia and to resist the German demands. Many people asked with apparently unassailable logic what would be the use of fighting a war if even in case of victory peace would have to be concluded on the basis of the German terms. It occurred to hardly anybody that what was presented by Lord Runciman as an axiom was in reality a false premise. Most people took it for granted that he was right in assuming that frontiers have to be fixed in accordance with ethnological considerations.

Yet even at the time of the Runciman report there was a very important precedent which proved that a solution on totally different lines would be possible. The example of the exchange of populations between Turkey and Greece proved that this solution is a much more suitable basis for securing peace and friendly relations than the acceptance of the ethno-

171

logical frontiers as the only possible basis for fixing
the political frontiers. Had Lord Runciman's principle been accepted at the Treaty of Lausanne, Greece
would have retained possession of the Smyrna district
and Greco-Turkish relations would have remained
unfriendly ever since. As, however, the Greek
minority which had lived around Smyrna for some
3000 years was resettled on Greek territory at the
cost of great sacrifices, Turkey and Greece have become
the best of friends.

Since the publication of the Runciman report
Hitler himself provided several examples for the
solution of minority problems without transfer of
territory. He agreed to the resettlement in Germany
of the German minorities in the Southern Tyrol, in
the Baltic States and in Bessarabia. He also ordered
the forcible ejection of solid blocks of Czechs and
Poles from territories which he wanted to populate
with Germans. The experience of the last two years
conclusively proved the fallacy of Runcimanism.
Evidently a solution on the lines of the resettlement
of the German minorities from Czecho-Slovakia would
have been possible and still is possible in case of
an Allied victory. The claim that the acceptance of
the German demand for fixing the political frontiers
along the ethnological frontiers was inevitable has
been amply disproved and Runcimanism has become
thoroughly discredited.

Nevertheless, a large number of people have come
to accept subconsciously the fundamental principle
of Runcimanism as applied in the economic sphere.
It is one of the trump cards of appeasers to declare
that since there is a solid block of eighty million
Germans in Central Europe it is necessary to adjust

the economic structure of Europe on the basis of that "unalterable" fact even in case of British victory, just as it was taken to be necessary to fix the frontiers of Czecho-Slovakia in case of Allied victory on the basis of the "unalterable" fact of the existence of solid blocks of German populations in the Sudeten districts. Beyond doubt, once the existence of a solid block of eighty million Germans is accepted as an unalterable basic fact, then the appeasers are in a position to argue with some convincing force that a nation of such a size is entitled to its living space. They can proceed along the lines of German propaganda which filled the ether and the world Press with its complaints before the war that while all other Great Powers had their *Grosswirtschaftsraum* (vast space on which the national economy can be displayed on a grand scale), poor Germany alone was confined within her own frontiers and was deprived of essential sources of raw materials. From this argument the appeasers inferred the conclusion that, given the fact that the eighty million Germans have to live, it is necessary to provide them with opportunities to live by enabling them to retain economic control over Eastern and South-Eastern Europe, and possibly also over other parts of the Continent. Consequently, even after a British victory it will become necessary, according to the appeasers, to satisfy Germany's claim for economic control over her living space.

The thesis of economic Runcimanism is presented with great emphasis in an article by Mr. C. W. Guillebaud appearing in the December 1940 issue of the *Economic Journal*. While professing to disapprove of Germany's bid for political domination of the European continent, he seeks to make out a case in

favour of economic domination of the Eastern and
South-Eastern States by Germany. To that end he
supports various aspects of Hitler's " New Order "
and seeks to convince his readers that were it not
for Hitler's bid for political domination the population
of Continental countries conquered by Germany
would stand to benefit by the Nazi economic doctrines
and by inter-European planning under German
leadership. He concludes that Central and Eastern
Europe, after we have won the war, will stand
in need of an economic order based on its own
necessities, and that the necessary organisation to
that end could only be undertaken by Germany.
"Nature and geographical facts", he continues,
" have placed Germany in the centre of a great area.
She has the industrial resources and the organising
ability which the other peoples of Eastern and South-
Eastern Europe lack and she is the natural market
for their products." To the objection that a Germany
which is put into the key position of supreme economic
organiser of Eastern and South-Eastern Europe will
inevitably be a strong Germany able once again to
make another bid for world domination, his answer
is that " no amount of wishful thinking would elimin-
ate Germany from the European scene ; she is there
a very solid and intractable fact and we have to work
out a way of living with her as a Great Power ".

So now we know how we stand. It is the supreme
task of post-war appeasement to create conditions
through the terms of the peace treaty by which
Germany shall retain a high degree of control over
a large part of the Continent and by which she shall
retain the position of a first-rate Power with the
means to plunge the world once more into destructive

war. Mr. Guillebaud and other appeasers present this
conclusion as a matter of historical determinism
against which it is useless and even impossible to
struggle. They contrive to convey the impression
to their readers that they are fated to put up with
a Germany which possesses all the means for their
destruction, and that their only hope for survival
lies in putting Germany in a conciliatory frame of
mind in the hour of victory by means of appeasement.

The effect of this economic Runcimanism tends to
be the same as was that of political Runcimanism
during the Czecho-Slovak crisis. If accepted by the
great majority of the nation, it will sap the will to
fight the war to a successful conclusion. Should the
argument put forward by Mr. Guillebaud and other
appeasers gain ground, a large and growing number
of people would ask themselves whether it is worth
while to continue fighting if in spite of further terrific
sacrifices the terms on which peace would eventually
be concluded would have to satisfy Germany's claims
and would have to leave her powerful and dangerous.

To dispose of this line of argument it is necessary
to make it plain that the presence in Central Europe
of a united German Empire of eighty million inhabitants is by no means an inevitable necessity ; that
it is not the duty of the future peacemakers to create
economic conditions which will enable the German
nation to remain united, powerful and dangerous ;
that the German peoples which are at present united
within the borders of the Third Reich are capable of
existing without the creation of an artificial economic
system such as envisaged by the appeasers ; and
finally, that it is not to the interest of the Eastern
and South-Eastern European nations that they should

willingly participate in any such scheme.

The experience of recent history has conclusively proved that the existence of a united Germany is against the interest of mankind. There is every justification for the victorious Allies to dismember the Reich into its component units. This political question will be dealt with in greater detail in the concluding chapter. In the present chapter we shall confine ourselves to examining the economic aspects of post-war appeasement.

Mr. Guillebaud and others seem to have accepted the German propaganda argument according to which a Great Power is entitled to a certain degree of control over the countries which it considers its *Lebensraum*. In reality, from a purely economic point of view, there is no case whatever for a differentiation in this respect between a Great Power and a small country. The problems of a nation of eight millions are essentially identical with those of a nation of eighty millions and the difference between them is merely one of degree. If a nation of eight millions is not self-sufficient it is confronted with the same problems as those faced by Germany, namely, to find markets for its exports in order that it should be able to import the essential goods which it is unable to produce at home.

Thus from a purely economic point of view a small nation such as Switzerland has as much or as little right as Germany to claim control over foreign countries in order to satisfy its economic requirements. To admit that there is a difference would amount to the admission of the law of the jungle, that the stronger nation has in law privileges to which the weaker nations are not entitled. Until the increase

of Germany's power under the Nazi régime no such
privileges were ever claimed or admitted. Great
Powers and small nations negotiated trade agreements
on an equal footing. Any small nation was fully
entitled to say " no " to commercial demands of a
Great Power, and the latter, in order to obtain the
condition it coveted, had to make it worth the small
nation's while to yield. The conception that small
nations because of their weakness should be degraded
into the *Lebensraum* of big nations is the logical outcome of the Nazi principle of " might is right ".

Even pre-1914 Germany with her immense military
power did not attempt putting forward and enforcing
a claim for economic control over countries which,
according to present-day phraseology, constituted
the *Lebensraum* of the Second Reich. Before 1914
Germany was making good progress in her trade
expansion over the Continent, and even in the complete absence of any specific privileges, let alone
economic control, she was able to secure the lion's
share in the trade of Eastern and South-Eastern
Europe. The contention that before 1914 Germany
was well on her way to achieving with peaceful
methods the ends which since 1939 she has sought to
achieve by war is, however, exaggerated, for in spite
of the progress of German trade expansion on the
Continent other nations had a fair chance to be
successful in certain countries and in certain trades.
It is true, nevertheless, that German trade expansion
on the Continent before 1914 secured for Germany the
satisfaction of her requirements. What matters is
that during that period Germany did not claim any
specific privileges but sought to gain ground by producing better and cheaper goods than her competitors

and by adapting herself to the requirements of her customers to a larger degree than her rivals. In other words, the German expansion before the last war was carried out with the aid of hard and honest work, and the success of that expansion proved that it is possible for Germany to achieve her legitimate ends with the aid of hard and honest work. It is true in the meantime a number of countries raised customs barriers against German goods, but experience proved that very few customs barriers are really prohibitive if Germany wants to penetrate into a market.

Thus even on the assumption that after her defeat Germany will be allowed to remain a united nation of eighty millions, it is entirely false to assume that consequently she must be given special privileges on the European continent, in order that her eighty million people should be able to live. Until the outbreak of the war Germany was able to trade with the five continents and was making progress in many overseas countries. Possibly her progress was not so spectacular as her expansion in South-Eastern Europe, but it was sufficiently evident to dispose of the argument that she had no scope for expansion outside the countries which she claimed as her *Lebensraum*. Her claim for a monopoly of South-Eastern European trade would have been justified if she had been excluded from markets outside that part of the world. Since, however, she was able to trade successfully with overseas countries there was no justification for her endeavours to exclude other countries from trade with South-Eastern Europe. The reason why it was considered a vital necessity for Germany to secure economic control over countries contiguous to her was of a purely military nature. Germany had reason to fear that in case of a war British naval blockade would cut her off from her overseas markets and supplies, and for this reason she sought to secure for herself the full use of the markets and sources of supply of countries contiguous to her. Thus Germany's *Lebensraum* claim formed part of her claim. for world domination. She needed economic control over her *Lebensraum* in order to be able to secure political control over it and over the rest of the world. From an economic point of view the *Lebensraum* argument was entirely untenable.

This being so, it is impossible to find justification for the satisfaction of Germany's *Lebensraum* claim after her defeat. She will be well in a position to trade again with overseas countries and to live, even without possessing a monopolistic position in Eastern and South-Eastern Europe. To suggest that the granting of such a monopolistic position to her is a vital necessity amounts to the admission that after her defeat Germany is entitled to begin immediately to prepare for the next war. It is only for the requirements of another war that she would need economic control over South-Eastern Europe. From a purely economic point of view it is quite as satisfactory for her to increase her overseas trade as to increase her trade with contiguous countries. The more she depends upon her overseas trade the less she is in a position to embark upon another war. The more she controls trade in Eastern and South-Eastern Europe the greater the temptation for her to attempt once more to achieve political domination.

In the circumstances it is unstatesmanlike to the extreme to suggest that the solution of the German problem lies in securing for her through the peace treaty the satisfaction of her economic ambitions in Eastern and South-Eastern Europe. Apart altogether from the political influence she would be able to bring to bear upon Eastern and South-Eastern Europe through the control of their trade, a high degree of self-sufficiency of the group of countries of which Germany would be made the centre would go a long way towards facilitating preparations for another war of aggression. It would be to the interest of peace that German trade should be diverted as much as possible to overseas countries and that non-German countries should secure the largest possible share in the trade of Eastern and South-Eastern Europe.

We have seen that from the point of view of peace economy the control of the countries which Germany claims to form part of her *Lebensraum* is by no means a necessity; and that from the point of view of securing lasting peace it would be a positive danger. There is, however, another powerful argument which has to be disposed of in order to discredit completely economic Runcimanism. It is the argument that the establishment of an economic unit in Central, Eastern and South-Eastern Europe under German control would be in accordance with the interests of the non-German members of this Federation. In support of this argument Mr. Guillebaud and others who share his views contend that the result of the economic nationalism that followed the conclusion of peace in 1919 was economic anarchy in Central and South-Eastern Europe; that the standard of living of the small countries in the Danube Basin and the Balkans declined in consequence; and that their salvation after the British victory lies in the voluntary adoption of some of the points of Hitler's " New Economic Order ".

To strengthen his case Mr. Guillebaud goes out of his way to endorse the claims of the German " New Order " propaganda, according to which the subject races would greatly benefit by the adoption of the " New Order ". For a detailed discussion of the arguments for and against the " New Order " I must refer the reader to my book *Hitler's " New Order " in Europe*. In that book I endeavoured to prove that the " New Order " would be an unmitigated evil from the point of view of the conquered countries as it would only serve the purposes of their exploitation by Germany. The outcome and the duration of the war largely depend upon the degree to which this truth is realised by the conquered peoples. It is therefore simply unforgivable that a British economist should go out of his way to support the " New Order " propaganda in an attempt to strengthen his thesis in favour of post-war appeasement. Mr. Guillebaud himself must have realised that by supporting the economic aspects of the " New Order " he placed himself in a false position. When I attacked his article in the January 11 issue of *Time and Tide*, Mr. Guillebaud in his answer disclaimed to have supported the " New Order ". In the course of the correspondence that developed in the columns of *Time and Tide* he was forced to admit, however, that he did recognise " the existence of certain great economic advantages which may be offered by the Hitler Plan ". Altogether his defence was characterised by a desire to have his cake and eat it. In order to make out a case in favour of German economic control over Eastern and South-Eastern Europe he was anxious to support at

N

least certain aspects of the " New Order ". On the other hand, he was equally anxious to avoid obtaining the reputation of being a supporter of the " New Order ". Nevertheless he committed himself in print to several statements which no amount of sophistry can explain away. He declared, for instance, in the *Economic Journal* that " France might stand to gain considerably in certain directions in the economic sphere through the application of the ' New Order ' ". He also declared that if Funk's agricultural scheme for South-Eastern Europe is successful it would have much to commend it.

Above all, Mr. Guillebaud sought to whitewash the " New Order " scheme of the charge that its sole aim was the exploitation of the subject races. " It would not be that type of Colonial exploitation that is so frequently cited by anti-Imperialists ", he declared in the course of an argument trying to show that in the long run it would be to Germany's interests to keep the subject races prosperous. These quotations suffice to show to what length appeasers are prepared to go in the interest of their policy of post-war appeasement. They seem to be unable to realise that since their endorsement of the " New Order " propaganda tends to weaken resistance to the " New Order " in occupied countries, the logical outcome of the success of their campaign would be a weakening of the chance for decisive British victory and the liberation of the conquered countries. To illustrate with an example the mischievous effect of appeasement propaganda, let it be sufficient to quote the case of Funk's agricultural claim endorsed by Mr. Guillebaud. In his speech of July 25, 1940, Funk promised the peasant population of South-Eastern Europe

steady markets and remunerative prices fixed in
advance for a long period. This offer is bound to be
tempting to the peasants in South-Eastern Europe,
especially after the difficulties during the early 'thirties
when they were unable to sell their products at remunerative prices. Whether or not the Nazi promises
will appeal depends, however, upon the degree to
which they believe in the sincerity of the promises.
If they can be made to realise that the monetary
manipulations which Germany will continue to pursue
in conquered countries tend to deprive them of the
advantages of high agricultural prices offered to them
by Germany, then Funk's offer will lose all its
appeal. Yet Mr. Guillebaud, and other writers
who have adopted the same attitude, go out of
their way to reassure the South-Eastern European
peoples that Nazi Germany has no intention of
exploiting them. In so far as their articles produce
an effect — and they were written for the purpose of
producing an effect — they could only have undermined the will of South-Eastern European countries
to resist Nazi domination.

In order to strengthen their case in favour of
German economic control of Eastern and South-
Eastern Europe after the war, Mr. Guillebaud and
others seek to paint an excessively unfavourable
picture of the economic effects of the peace treaties
in that part of the world. Mr. Guillebaud maintained
that largely owing to the growth of population in
Eastern and South-Eastern Europe their standard of
living has been falling since the end of the last war
and is now lower than it was before 1914. His proposed remedy is to bolster up agricultural prices
in Eastern and South-Eastern Europe through the

application of Funk's agricultural scheme. In reality
there is a much more natural solution of the problem
of over-population, namely the development of certain
industries. From the point of view of the Eastern
and South-Eastern European countries it would be
much more satisfactory to increase the purchasing
power of the population through industrialisation
than to depend upon Germany's willingness to buy
up their products at artificially high prices. There
is ample justification for the development of many
branches of industries, especially of those connected
with agriculture in Eastern and South-Eastern Europe.
This is, however, strongly against the fundamental principles of the " New Order " and of post-war economic
appeasement.

One of the principal aims of the " New Order "
is to stamp out in the conquered countries any
branches of production which are superfluous from
the point of view of German interests. Admittedly
our appeasers do not actually endorse this brutal
formula. Mr. Guillebaud in his article pays lip-service
to the necessity of taking into consideration the rights
and interests of all the peoples involved. Nevertheless, in substance his scheme would amount to persuading the Eastern and South-Eastern European
countries that they should voluntarily adapt their
economic systems to Germany's requirements, very
much on the same lines as they would be forced to
adapt them under the " New Order " if Germany
should win the war. Yet it is obvious that even if
Germany were prepared to pay genuinely high prices
for Eastern and South-Eastern European agricultural
products, it would be more in accordance with the
interests of the countries concerned to make produc-

tive use of their surplus of man-power through the development of industries. This would not necessarily mean that they would cease to trade with Germany. Before the war the value of British goods sold to Germany per head of the population was many times larger than the corresponding figure for India. This in spite of the fact that British exports had a privileged position in India while they were sought to be limited and excluded by every possible means in Germany, simply because industrialised Germany had incomparably higher purchasing power than agricultural India. Industrialisation would increase the purchasing power of Eastern and South-Eastern Europe and would enable them to buy German goods, even though the lines in demand would not necessarily remain the same.

From the foregoing it is clear that it would be contrary to the interests of Eastern and South-Eastern European countries to agree voluntarily to become part of Germany's *Lebensraum*. The contention of economic Runcimanism that Eastern and South-Eastern Europe is bound to come under German economic control and that it is to the interest of the countries concerned that this should be so is as false as its contention that the eighty million Germans in Central Europe cannot live unless they are allowed to secure economic control over Eastern and South-Eastern Europe.

CHAPTER XV

ONE of the favourite arguments in support of appeasement is that it would be possible to undermine the
loyalty of the German nation to Hitler by promising
that Great Britain will be generous to Germany after
victory or in case of a compromise peace, provided
that she will discard the Nazi régime. This argument is based on a total misunderstanding of the
attitude of the German people towards its Fuehrer.
In this respect there is more wishful thinking than
in any other respect in this war, which is saying a
great deal. At the beginning of the war the majority
of British public opinion, and even official opinion,
was convinced that the German nation was following
Hitler with the utmost reluctance in his reckless
adventure, and that it would be sufficient to drop
a few pamphlets to bring about an armed revolt
leading to the overthrow of the Nazi régime. Others,
less sanguine, were convinced that the pamphlets
would at any rate lead to passive resistance and would
weaken the German war effort. Consequently, while
Warsaw was being reduced to ruins by the German
Air Force, the Government of Mr. Chamberlain confined itself to pamphlet raids over Germany. The
only effect of these raids was to reduce to some slight
extent the paper shortage prevailing in Germany.
Admittedly the pamphlets were as badly worded as
they could possibly be, but even if they had been

as good as they were bad it would not have made the slightest difference to the attitude of the German nation.

It is sad but true that in this war the Germans are behind Hitler to an even larger degree than they were behind the Kaiser during the last war. Between 1914 and 1918 there was at least a feeble opposition to the war but now for all practical purposes it is simply non-existent. The extent of Hitler's popularity in Germany was not realised by those who believed that a few pamphlets dropped by an enemy Power could lead to his overthrow. He succeeded in winning the enthusiastic support of practically the entire German nation first by creating steady employment and then by scrapping the Treaty of Versailles. As I pointed out in earlier chapters, though that Treaty inflicted very little genuine hardship upon the German people, German propaganda during the Weimar Republic, and even more under the Nazi régime, succeeded in working up a sweeping feeling that Germany had been made the victim of grave injustice and ruthless oppression. It is no wonder that the man who wrecked the Versailles system was looked upon as the redeemer of the German nation by at least ninety-nine Germans out of a hundred.

In particular at the moment of the German victory over Poland it was simply absurd to think that Hitler's popularity could be undermined. The Polish Corridor separating Eastern Prussia from the rest of the Reich had been considered as the most iniquitous clause of the Treaty of Versailles, and the Poles had always been regarded as the most hated and most detested amongst Germany's enemies. Their crushing defeat within a few weeks at the cost of negligible sacrifices would in itself have been sufficient for establishing Hitler's popularity even amongst anti-Nazis in Germany.

Moreover, by that time the German people discovered that war can be made to become a paying proposition if the victor is ruthless enough in exploiting his victim. Ever since the bloodless occupation of Prague the loot was simply pouring into Germany from Czecho-Slovakia and many Germans were given in the conquered provinces lucrative posts far beyond their most sanguine anticipations. The occupation troops were sending parcels to their families, and residents within reasonable distance from the frontier crossed into Czecho-Slovakia for highly beneficial foraging expeditions. The same experience repeated itself of course after the conquest of Poland, with the difference that while in Czecho-Slovakia outward forms were sought to be maintained, Poland was openly treated as Germany's Plunderland.

With the lightning conquest of Denmark, Norway, the Low Countries and France, Hitler enhanced considerably both the laurels earned in Poland and the sordid material benefit derived by the German people from the pillaging of its victims. Foodstuffs were simply pouring into Germany from the conquered countries and the occupation troops were living on the fat of the land. This consideration, even more than the decisive defeat of the hereditary enemy across the Rhine at the cost of relatively negligible sacrifices, enhanced Hitler's prestige and popularity in Germany to a degree that could hardly be exaggerated.

It was at this stage that the German propaganda machine came out with the " New Order " scheme.

While for foreign consumption Hitler's " New Order in Europe " was presented as a scheme which was devised for the benefit of conqueror and conquered alike, for home consumption the Nazi leaders admitted with cynical candour that Europe was meant to be made into a vast Plunderland for the benefit of the ruling race. German workmen were given to understand that once the war was over their lot will be an enviable one. All the inferior work would be performed with the aid of foreign slave labour and the workmen of the ruling race would be paid generous wages. In the circumstances it is not surprising that the German workmen should regard with approval and even with enthusiasm Hitler's endeavours to consolidate the conquest of Europe by the defeat of Great Britain. It is doubtful whether many members of the German working classes lose sleep over the thought that their standard of living would be raised at the cost of the workmen of the subject races.

Apart from such materialistic considerations the majority of the German people thoroughly enjoy the glory of Germany having become the centre of a most powerful empire with good prospects for achieving world domination. This point of view is not adequately understood in left-wing circles in Great Britain who have little use for the idea of the British Empire. Even those who do not share their views are inclined to be rather *blasé* about it, because British people have for long been accustomed to being in control of a world empire. The German people, on the other hand, having lost their preponderant position in Europe and in the world through the outcome of the Thirty Years' War, and having declined to a very low depth after their defeat in

1918, are apt to regard with enthusiasm their newly created powerful empire. It is like a new toy to children, and most Germans simply worship Hitler for having raised Germany within the space of a few brief years to the highest position she has ever occupied since the time of Charlemagne.

Even to-day Frenchmen hold the memory of Napoleon in great reverence for the passing glory he brought to France. It is no wonder that German people should feel in the same way about Hitler who achieved greater power in a shorter time and with much less sacrifice than Napoleon.

To appreciate the extent of the cult of Hitler in Germany it is also useful to recall that the Libyan victories at the end of 1940 and the beginning of 1941 led to the development within a few weeks of a very marked cult of General Wavell in Great Britain. Well-deserved as his popularity is, the extent of his victories bears no comparison with those won by Hitler in Eastern, Northern, Western and Southern Europe. Moreover, the Germans are essentially a martial race and are more liable than the peace-loving British to appreciate military victories and conquests.

This is the truth about the attitude of the German nation towards Hitler, and unpalatable as it is, it should be realised in order to avoid embarking upon a policy based upon entirely false premises.

In the circumstances it is utterly futile to hope that the German people could be detached from Hitler if only the British Government were to promise them generous treatment if they should overthrow the Nazi régime. For one thing the predominant majority of the German nation does not believe in the possibility of a British victory. Having witnessed the unprecedented success of the German arms in every part of the Continent, they are convinced that Germany under Hitler is invincible. The majority of the German people firmly believe that sooner or later the British resistance will be overcome, or at any rate that the war will result in a draw, leaving Hitler in undisturbed possession of his conquests on the Continent. This being so, it is idle to expect them to pay much heed to promises made in case of a British victory.

Moreover, it ought to be borne in mind that the present generation in Germany has been brought up on anti-Versailles propaganda, the main point of which was the denunciation of the Allies for having violated the pledges given in President Wilson's Fourteen Points. Needless to say, in this respect as in every other respect, the German propaganda against the Treaty of Versailles has been wildly exaggerated. There is hardly anyone in Germany, however, who would not endorse the German charge against the Allies that they had induced Germany to surrender with the aid of promises which were dishonoured once Germany was disarmed and helpless. In such circumstances there would be very few people in Germany who would take British promises of generous treatment at their face value.

Another reason why the German people would disbelieve in British promises of generous treatment lies in its consciousness of its own guilt. During the last war the atrocities committed against Allied populations and shipping were strenuously denied in German official circles for fear of their effect upon neutral opinion. In this war German propaganda both for home and for foreign consumption goes out of its way to boast of the terrorising methods employed, in the hope of intimidating into surrender those who might otherwise be inclined to resist. The details of the destructions caused in Warsaw, Rotterdam and London through indiscriminate bombing are given with much relish. It is openly admitted that the machine-gunning of civilian refugees in Flanders and France formed part of Hitler's plan of intimidation. That plan aimed at increasing the horrors of war to such an extent that the opponent would have to sue for peace. Thus it is expected that, at the cost of the extermination of some hundreds of thousands of women and children, the lives of hundreds of thousands of German soldiers can be spared. Human nature being what it is, the Germans are inclined to judge others by themselves. They are fully aware that they themselves would never forgive an opponent for inflicting such suffering upon them, and that as soon as they had gained the upper hand they would wreak ruthless vengeance upon the defeated foe. They take it for granted that this is exactly what the British nation intends to do in case of victory. Consequently they are firmly convinced that Germany must win the war in order that they should be spared the British vengeance. For this reason alone they would give Hitler their utmost support.

In any case, what is it that British propaganda could possibly offer which would tempt the German people into deserting Hitler ? Even the most generous peace terms would naturally leave Germany in a less satisfactory condition than she would be in in case of German victory. Even if Mr. Guillebaud's claim for German economic control over Eastern and South-Eastern Europe were to be adopted as the basis of official British propaganda, the compromise would hardly appeal to the German people which in case of victory would have the full control of the resources of Eastern and South-Eastern Europe and the rest of the European continent. The *Herrenvolk* can hardly be expected to be enthusiastic about a limited exploitation of part of Europe if it is at present in a position to exploit to the full practically the whole of continental Europe.

Admittedly, in addition to generous peace terms there is something else which the German people can be offered in case of British victory. It is the restoration of their freedom under a democratic régime. It is a mistake to imagine, however, that the German people are likely to grow enthusiastic at the prospect. The democratic régime did not work too satisfactorily in Germany between 1918 and 1933. Admittedly it never had a fair test, but people judge by results. In the minds of most Germans the democratic régime is associated with political and economic instability, with wholesale inflation and wholesale unemployment. In any case, the ideals of democracy and freedom are by no means so precious to the average German as to the average Englishman. The Germans are an essentially disciplinarian race. They like to obey rather than take a part in shaping their own destinies. They like to bow to authority and they have the greatest admiration for the display of a strong hand. If left-wing appeasers, judging others by themselves, imagine that their promises of freedom and democracy to the German people carry much weight it is because they ignore one of the fundamental characteristics of the German race.

Conceivably this state of affairs may change

slightly if the war should become prolonged and if the full participation of the United States should make the German people realise that there can be no question of an early victory. The food reserves and other capital assets of conquered countries cannot be looted twice, and if the British and Allied forces succeed in calling a halt to the German march of triumph, the *Herrenvolk* will cease to enjoy the benefit derived from wholesale lootings. The exploitation of the conquered races would of course continue to secure for Germany substantial advantages, but the increasing requirements of the war would more than absorb the surplus obtained from conquered territories. Even though the standard of living of the *Herrenvolk* would be kept well above that of the subject races, it would have to decline as and when the naval blockade becomes watertight and Germany's means of production are gradually reduced through air bombing. Even then it would take a long time before the cooling of German enthusiasm for Hitler could reach a sufficiently advanced stage to make a difference in practice to the extent of their support. There would be a growing volume of grumbling but the predominant majority of Germans would remain strictly loyal so long as there appeared to be a chance left for German victory.

It is not until British victory becomes obviously imminent that the Germans are likely to change their attitude towards Hitler. Then and only then the final collapse could conceivably be hastened by a few weeks through promises of immunity from punishment in case of the overthrow of the Nazi régime. But by that time the days of that régime would be numbered in any case, and it would be bad statesmanship for

Great Britain to limit her freedom of action at the peace conference for the sake of shortening the war by a few weeks.

Another popular argument used in an effort to induce the Government to commit itself to lenient treatment of defeated Germany is that it would secure for the Allies the support of anti-Nazi Germans living abroad. As a matter of fact the predominant majority of Aryan Germans in foreign countries is organised on Nazi lines and gives its wholehearted support to Hitler. The number of pure Aryan Germans who because of their anti-Nazi political creed have given their support to the Allied cause is really negligible, and it would be absurd if consideration for this infinitesimal fraction should be allowed to influence major decisions of fundamental policy.

On the other side of the balance-sheet it is necessary to take into consideration the effect of a policy of appeasement in favour of Germany upon the attitude of the conquered races. I have already dealt with this subject at some length in Chapter XIV, but there are a few additional points which may be worth considering.

Generally speaking it is unfortunately true that the extent of collaboration of the conquered races with the occupation authorities is much higher in this war than in the last war. During the last war the territories conquered by Germany were a liability rather than an asset from the point of view of her economic war effort. While she was able to derive benefit from the reconstructed Rumanian oil wells and from the Lorraine iron ore production, generally speaking the collaboration of the conquered peoples was negligible. Their attitude was sullen and entirely passive. In the hope of their liberation through the victory of the Allies they were prepared to face extreme privations rather than work for the hated conqueror. The same cannot be said to be true during the present war. Even in Poland where the extent of collaboration is considerably less than in any other conquered country millions of workmen are engaged in tasks that tend to contribute towards Germany's economic war effort. In Czecho-Slovakia the Skoda works produce tanks by the thousand for the German Army, and it was these tanks which broke through the French lines in 1940, thereby postponing considerably the liberation of Czecho-Slovakia. In Denmark, France and even Belgium the people have settled down to a high degree of collaboration with Germany. The Norwegian and Dutch peoples displayed more resistance, but even in their case the degree of collaboration is incomparably higher than that of the countries conquered by Germany during the last war.

The explanation of this unsatisfactory state of affairs is twofold. During the last war it was taken for granted that the conquered territories would be liberated within a relatively short time. During this war, especially after the surprisingly quick collapse of France, defeatism seized the conquered peoples. Even though the successful resistance of Great Britain raised new hopes, it is widely believed in conquered countries that it will take a long time before joint British-American effort would succeed in effecting their liberation. In spite of this there would be a higher degree of passive and even active resistance, were it not for very widespread fears that even a

British and Allied victory would only mean temporary and partial removal of German control. While the German people are convinced that the British terms in case of British victory would be harsh to the extreme, the conquered peoples, on the other hand, fear that those terms would be much too lenient and would leave them at the mercy of Germany.

The agitation of British appeasers naturally tends to increase these fears amongst the conquered peoples, and to that extent it tends to stimulate their collaboration with the conqueror. In particular the agitation in favour of allowing Germany to retain economic control over the whole or part of the Continent tends to encourage economic collaboration between conqueror and conquered. This is only natural. Many people in the conquered countries are inclined to abstain from helping Germany in her economic war effort, and nothing short of acute threat of starvation induces them to collaborate very reluctantly and half-heartedly. Their half-heartedness naturally tends to affect the results of their work. If, on the other hand, they are told on the authority of British economists and politicians that even in case of British victory they have to resign themselves to remaining Germany's *Lebensraum* and that they are, so to speak, abandoned economically in favour of Germany, it is only natural that many of them should arrive at the conclusion that, this being so, there can be no harm in beginning to collaborate straight away.

The mischievous effects of that false historical determinism with the aid of which appeasers seek to convey the impression that, irrespective of the outcome of the war, the continental nations are fated to accept close collaboration with Germany under

German control are only too obvious. It is no wonder that the various " free " Governments established in London are doing their utmost to fight against this attitude. Those left-wing appeasers who agitate in favour of holding a conference with these free Governments to arrive at peace terms by agreement with these Governments would be surprised if they knew the sort of peace terms that would emerge from such a conference. Indeed, were it not for the fact that these Governments wish to follow the British lead in abstaining from defining in public their attitude towards peace aims they would not make a secret of their demand for terms of the utmost severity, in order to safeguard their countries from being re-conquered by Germany. The impression I gained through my contact with the Allied Free Governments in London is that, although there may be a marked difference in the degree of severity which the various Allied politicians advocated even the mildest formula suggested by any of them was sufficiently drastic to show the feelings among the London representatives of the Allied peoples. On the rare occasions when some of the Allied statesmen express their views about peace aims in public statements — for instance, in March 1941 the Dutch Prime Minister declared himself in favour of a " hard " peace — the " appeasement Press " either ignores them or condenses their statement to a few non-committal lines.

Yet from the point of view of the strength of the support of the various free Governments it would be highly salutary if the British Government were to come out openly in favour of peace terms which would safeguard the liberated countries against a

fresh German aggression. The result of such a statement of policy would be that the nationals of the
countries concerned who live abroad would consider
it worth their while to give the maximum of support
in the hope that once their nations are liberated their
freedom would not be endangered by a revival of the
German peril. As it is, the doubts about Great
Britain's ultimate intentions must have played quite
a considerable part in inducing many supporters of
the various free Governments, especially of the Free
French Government, to return to their native lands
and submit to German control.

Admittedly, the declaration of the Government's
policy to impose a peace upon Germany which would
deprive her of the chances of repeating 1914 and 1939
would be a direct challenge to woolly sentimentalism
in Great Britain and the United States. Even so,
the advantages of this course would heavily outweigh
its disadvantages. Those who maintain that a
decision to enforce a hard peace against Germany
would split the nation may be right. The proportion
of those who would be antagonised by such a decision
to such an extent as to affect their war effort would
be, however, a bare fraction of one per cent of the
total population. It is true that this minority is
a very vocal one and would make enough noise to
convey the impression that a substantial proportion
of the nation is behind them. Nevertheless, their
agitation would make very little practical difference
in terms of the economic and military war effort.
Should the Government be ill-advised enough to
follow their suggestion and declare itself in favour of
a " soft " peace, the detrimental effect upon the war
effort would be incomparably larger. A very consider-

able proportion of the British people would then come to the conclusion that it is hardly worth while to win this war if Germany is given a chance to try it again shortly, for the odds would be overwhelmingly against this country also winning the next war. This feeling is very widely held among the Armed Forces and also among the civilian population of those towns which experience particularly heavy air raids. All these people would be heartened to a considerable extent by a declaration of the Government in favour of " hard " peace, and the increase of their efforts would probably make up for the decline of that of the advocates of a " soft " peace.

The same may be said to be true also concerning the United States, though not perhaps to the same extent. Being thousands of miles away from the scene of hostilities, many Americans imagine they can afford to be generous and forgiving. American public opinion is still at the phase where British opinion was at the time of Munich. It is, however, making considerable progress in the right direction and at the present rate a stage will soon be reached when it will be possible to ignore woolly sentimentalism in the United States as in Great Britain.

There is therefore everything to be said in favour of an early statement of peace aims by the Government, though not in the sense in which it is being pressed to declare itself. A declaration in favour of " hard " peace could not possibly increase the German nation's support for Hitler. That support is already very nearly a hundred per cent. On the other hand, it would considerably increase the active support of the Allied cause by the peoples of conquered countries. This is a factor of first-rate importance, for if collaboration between the conquered peoples and their conqueror should continue on the present scale, their liberation would become an extremely lengthy, difficult, and possibly even impossible task. While admittedly the success of the British arms would be the best propaganda in conquered territories, its effect could be extensively supplemented and even substituted by giving the conquered peoples emphatic assurances that after British victory they would not be left at Germany's mercy.

CHAPTER XVI

AN ALTERNATIVE TO THE " NEW ORDER "

THE policy of appeasement is built upon the dogmatic belief in the fundamental goodness of the German people. Those who profess this policy in good faith hold the view that if only the Germans are treated in a conciliatory way they would cease to be a menace to world peace. There is not a scrap of concrete evidence in support of this contention. On the contrary, all the evidence produced by history is emphatically against it. It is clear that mere change in the régime of Germany is not sufficient to bring about a fundamental change in German character that would provide adequate safeguards against the pursuit of aggressive designs. After the defeat of the German Army in 1918 Germany changed her régime in the hope that through this eleventh-hour change she would escape the consequences of her support given to the Imperialistic and aggressive régime of the Kaiser. The moderates who took charge from 1918 never enjoyed, however, adequate support by the nation. Indeed, if they were genuinely moderate like Erzberger or Rathenau they were assassinated and their assassins escaped punishment. The moderate régime was only able to maintain its precarious control over Germany while it was evident that the restoration of an aggressive régime would mean French invasion. The moment France loosened her grip the German nation chose once more a régime according to its heart's desire.

The argument that had the Treaty of Versailles been more lenient the moderates would have been able to consolidate their position is thus contradicted by the indisputable facts of the history of the post-war period. Let us for the sake of argument assume that the opposite contention according to which this war could have been avoided had the peace treaty been much harsher than it was is not proved. It stands to reason, however, that everything depends upon the degree of harshness and thoroughness with which a defeated Germany is deprived of the means for repeating her acts of aggression. Admittedly, if the assumption of the appeasers about the fundamental goodness of the German people is correct, then such harsh treatment would inflict injustice upon the nation. On the other hand, if the appeasers' assumption should prove to be wrong, then the acceptance of their views would lead to another war, and this time Germany may succeed in her attempt at world domination. In the circumstances, it seems preferable to risk being unjust to a nation of eighty millions — which by its past behaviour would have largely itself to blame for this — rather than risk German domination over Europe and the world. If the choice lies between eighty million Germans and four hundred million non-German Europeans — and even some sixteen hundred million non-German inhabitants of the globe — then obviously the smaller risk of being unjust to the German nation must be chosen in preference to the incomparably bigger risk.

Many people, while freely admitting Germany's war guilt on many occasions in history, claim that if only on this occasion she were treated leniently after her defeat the leopard would change its spots. This belief shows very much similarity to Mr. Chamberlain's acceptance of Hitler's word in Munich and his belief that even though he may have broken his word many times before, this time he would honour it.

The appeasers, in order to carry conviction, are trying their best to make our flesh creep by fore-casting the disastrous prospects that would follow the rejection of their views. They maintain that unless Germany is treated in the way that they want her to be treated, another war twenty years after the end of this war would become inevitable. The answer to this should be that if we should follow their advice another war would be inevitable not in twenty years but in five years.

It is also often argued even by people who tempera-mentally do not belong to the school of appeasers that it would be idle to try to enforce a harsh peace against Germany, for the sentimentalism and misguided humanitarianism of the British nation would not stand for it for any length of time. Even though it would be possible to fix the terms of peace on the basis of inflicting upon Germany the punishment she so richly deserves, in five years' time the British people would insist upon the relaxation of the control imposed upon her. And since just about that time the German nation would begin to recover from the wounds inflicted upon it by defeat, the relaxation of control over it would provide an opportunity of building up once more its power for evil.

Even on the assumption that this contention is correct, the world would gain five years of peace, for Germany would only resume her warlike preparations

five years after her defeat instead of immediately.
Moreover, during the period of control it would be
possible to take extensive measures as a result of
which even after the removal of control it would be
extremely difficult for her to rearm in haste. Consequently, even if the worst came to the worst, harsh
treatment of Germany would prolong the period of
peace that will follow this war.

Opponents of Hitler's " New Order " are often
accused by the apologists of that system that their
attitude is purely negative. For while rejecting and
discrediting Hitler's scheme they are unable to put
forward an alternative solution. Needless to say,
the " New Order " scheme is such an unmitigated
evil that even the return of the pre-war system would
be a hundred per cent improvement. Nevertheless,
it would be an error to allow apologists of the " New
Order " to convey the impression that there is no
constructive alternative to the " New Order ". For
the pre-war state of affairs was very far from satisfactory and the propaganda value of advocating a
fundamental change should not be underrated.

There is indeed an alternative to Hitler's " New
Order " and that is the application of an inverted
" New Order ". That is, all the principles which
Germany seeks to apply for the sake of securing and
consolidating her domination over Europe and subsequently over the rest of the world should be applied
against her. An extreme application of this formula
would imply a treatment of the German people
similar to the one inflicted by her upon the unfortunate Poles. According to this, since Germany has
embarked systematically upon the extermination of
the Polish race, there is every justification to put the

Poles in charge of the German nation and allow them a free hand to repay with interest for all they suffered under German domination. This would mean the reduction of the German population by mass executions, starvation, eviction from their homes during winter, wholesale sterilisation, etc. It would mean the seizure of their food supplies and the curtailment of their productive activities unless they benefited their conquerors. It would be difficult to object on moral grounds to such an extreme solution considering that Germany has been applying such ruthless measures and would do so once more on an even more extensive scale if she were given a chance. From a practical point of view, it is beyond doubt that there are far too many Germans in the world and that it would be to the interest of mankind if by some means their number could be materially reduced. Nevertheless, it seems certain that in spite of the sufferings which the British nation had to undergo in this war it will not stand for such a solution in the hour of victory. On the ground of this assumption the appeasers argue that since the German nation cannot be exterminated it must be appeased by means of far-reaching concessions. Those who are opposed to their policy are accused of lacking a sense of reality.

Fortunately it is possible to put forward an alternative programme for the curtailment of Germany's power for evil which would be acceptable to the British nation. Admittedly, it would not offer a hundred per cent safeguard against another war of aggression by Germany. Nothing short of the extermination of rather more than half the eighty million Germans would offer such a safeguard. Since such a solution must be ruled out, we must aim at a solution which is likely to appeal to the British nation and at the same time removes to a considerable degree the chances of another war.

In the political sphere the dismemberment of the Reich after its defeat appears to be an imperative necessity. The larger units which composed Germany before 1871 should be restored to their former independence. There should be an independent Austria, Bavaria, Würtemberg, Baden, Saxony, etc. There should also be a buffer State in the Rhineland, since the acquisition of this territory by Prussia was comparatively recent and its population is not typically Prussian. The ruling dynasties in these various States should be restored since many of them have still followers, and their presence would to some extent consolidate the independence of these Germanic States from Prussia.

There should be, of course, a complete military occupation of Germany after the war, but while in the case of the independent States detached from the Reich this military occupation should be only temporary, in the case of Prussia it may have to be permanent. By her unscrupulous aggressive attitude ever since the time of Frederick the Great, Prussia has forfeited the right to be an independent State.

In this respect as in respect of the dismemberment of the Reich, some of the principles which a victorious Germany would apply to Europe should be applied to her.

In the economic sphere, too, the solution lies in the application against Germany of the inverted principles of the " New Order ". The aim of the " New Order " is to make Germany into the arsenal and workshop of Europe and to de-industrialise the subject races whose rôle would be confined to producing the goods which are needed by Germany and to supplying slave labour for German industries. Accordingly defeated Germany should be de-industralised to a considerable degree. All the war-material-producing industries should be stamped out and industries which could be converted for the production of war materials, or even for the production of machinery necessary for war-material industries, should be restricted and placed under Allied supervision. Germany should also be deprived as far as possible of the means of producing essential raw materials and fuel required for the conduct of a war. Her synthetic oil plants and her oil refineries should be dismantled so that she should be dependent upon the import of refined oil products.

The de-industrialisation of Germany would reduce her requirements for railway and road facilities, and accordingly the capacity of some of the strategically important lines of communication should be reduced. In order to provide employment for the large number of German workmen who thus become released, they should be conscripted and should be placed in charge of the reconstruction of devastations inflicted by Germany upon other countries. When this task is completed, the conscript German labour should be employed for the construction of lines of fortifications in countries which in the past were subject to German aggression. German conscript labour should also be employed permanently as unskilled labour. The democratic countries will have to maintain permanently large and well-equipped armies as a safeguard of peace and the German conscript labour would thus replace the man-power which is thus tied

down. All this is in accordance with the principles
worked out by Germany for the benefit of her victims,
with the difference that German conscript labourers
would be treated as human beings. It is Germany's
intention in case of victory to develop the ruling race
into a race of warriors and superior workmen and to
use the millions of workmen of the subject races for
all inferior works. This plan can and should work
also in the opposite sense. Germany should supply
the man-power to take the place of the men who
have to be kept permanently under arms in order
to safeguard the world against a revival of her
aggressive designs.

There is ample scope also for a reversal of the
Lebensraum principle. The main purpose of Hitler's
" New Economic Order " is to adapt the economies
of countries contiguous to Germany to Germany's
economic requirements. The inversion of this principle would imply the reduction within the limits of
possibility of the extent to which these countries
complete Germany's economic system. This would
be in accordance with the interests and security of
the countries concerned. If they are unable to
produce what Germany needs, Germany will have
less means and less inducement for reconquering them.

To give a concrete example, the elimination of
Rumania's oil supplies would go a long way towards
reducing the extent to which Germany could rely
upon South-Eastern Europe for her war requirements.
This end could be achieved by the accelerated exploitation of Rumania's oil resources immediately after the
war, irrespective of commercial considerations. In
any case the Rumanian oil deposits are believed to be
approaching exhaustion and their increased exploita-

tion by Germany during the war will go a long way towards bringing their exhaustion nearer. In collaboration with Rumania, the Allied Governments should spare no effort to achieve the removal of Rumania from the ranks of the principal oil-producing countries. This, together with the dismantling of synthetic oil plants and refineries, would make it extremely difficult for Germany to embark upon another war of aggression.

To give another example, the production of soya beans in various South-Eastern European countries which was introduced and encouraged by Germany during the last few pre-war years and during the war should be discontinued. Let Germany depend upon imports from Manchukuo and other distant lands. From an economic point of view it is a very perverted arrangement indeed that soya beans should be produced in countries whose natural conditions are less suitable for the purpose than those of Manchukuo, and where labour is incomparably more expensive. There is no justification whatever for agitating in favour of bolstering up such an artificial arrangement. If Germany wishes to remain at peace, it is much more satisfactory for her to import soya beans by the sea route from Manchukuo than to have them grown in South-Eastern Europe. If in spite of this she developed the production of soya beans in South-Eastern Europe, it was solely in the interest of her war economy and solely with the purpose of assisting her in the task of achieving world domination. Those who maintain that after this war South-Eastern Europe should be made to continue to supply Germany with soya beans are, unwittingly or otherwise, in favour of enabling Germany to prepare for the next war.

We saw in Chapter XII that it would be in accordance with the interests of South-Eastern European
countries that they should achieve a certain degree
of industrialisation. By such means they would
cease to be dependent to an excessive degree upon
manufacture imports from Germany, though their
increased prosperity would enable them to import
luxuries from her. As for German exports, markets
should be reserved for them in overseas countries and
her requirements of oil and other raw materials
should also be satisfied by overseas countries.

The result of this system would be that Germany
would depend for her vital supplies upon the continuity of her overseas trade. This in itself would
not place her at a grave disadvantage in time of peace
but would materially increase her difficulties in time
of war. Therefore it would be an effective deterrent
for her to embark upon another war.

It is of course inevitable that all these measures
should bring about a reduction in the standard of
living in Germany. She would have to revert to
agriculture to an increasing extent and one of her
important sources of income would be the remittances
of her conscript labourers employed abroad. Such
remittances, together with the absence of any standing
army and any military and police expenditure which
would be borne by the Allied occupation authorities,
would mitigate the extent of the decline in her
standard of living. Even so, on balance there would
be a decline. On the other hand, the German people
would derive compensation for this decline by the
assurance that their leaders would not be allowed
once more to plunge Germany into a war and to
exploit her for the purposes of rearmament. This

may be small comfort for a generation brought up in the belief that Germany is the ruling race in the world. But here again the argument which is freely applied by German propaganda in an effort to make the " New Order " palatable to the subject races would recoil upon the German nation.

Considering that the alternative to this inevitable reduction in the German standard of living would be the risk of another war, it would be absurd to object to it on humanitarian grounds. It would be equally absurd to object to it on the ground that the world would lose trade if eighty million Germans were to become less prosperous. No amount of trade with Germany could compensate the world for the higher risk of another war. Considerations of security against another German aggression must overrule every other consideration.

The above alternative to the " New Order " is admittedly far from being an ideal solution. But then we do not live in an ideal world and there can be no ideal solution. The choice lies between two sets of disadvantages and risks. The inverted " New Order " would certainly reduce the risk of another war to a considerable extent by methods which may appear drastic in comparison with the Treaty of Versailles but which are incomparably more humane than those imposed by Germany upon her victims.

To a large extent the execution of the inverted " New Order " scheme would necessitate planning both on a national and international scale. For instance, the employment of German conscript labour should be carried through without causing unemployment in the countries where that labour is used. After the last war the French Government objected

to the reconstruction of French devastated areas by
German labour on the ground that this would be to
the detriment of French labour and French industries.
This is undoubtedly true under a system of *laissez-
faire*. Under a planned system, however, French
labour and industries could be fully employed for the
production of goods for current requirements, and
the admission of German conscript labour would
obviate the necessity for reducing the standard of
living in order to reconstruct the property destroyed.
After the completion of the work of reconstruction
judicious planning would find permanent scope for
German conscript labour without thereby displacing
national labour in the countries concerned.

The chances are that there will be no need for
maintaining permanent control over the non-Prussian
German States. In all probability they would settle
down to peaceful activities and their nationals would
realise that, once they have abandoned their world-
conquering ambitions, they could work out a satisfactory existence. Even in Prussia it is conceivable
that in the course of time Allied control would mollify
that arrogant spirit and unbridled ambition which
has been responsible for so much destruction and
suffering.

The realisation that it is not always possible after
a defeat to carry out a rearmament such as was
witnessed between 1933 and 1939 may in itself go a
long way towards discouraging the warlike spirit in
Prussia. It is perhaps possible to hope without undue
optimism that sooner or later even the Prussian nation
could take its place among the free and equal nations
working towards the betterment of mankind.

POSTSCRIPT

THE German attack on Soviet Russia has in many respects changed the situation from the point of view of appeasement. Its immediate result was the almost complete cessation of Left-wing appeasement agitation. So long as the Soviet Union continues to resist, British Communists and most Left-wing Socialists are likely to remain opposed to any peace of compromise with Hitler's Germany. Should the German invaders succeed, however, in overcoming the resistance of the Red Army, the chances are that Left-wing appeasers will resume their efforts.

Should, on the other hand, Russia succeed in defeating the German invaders, or even checking their progress, there is good reason to expect an increase of Right-wing agitation in favour of appeasement. Had it not been for Mr. Churchill's prompt and emphatic statement in favour of aid to Soviet Russia immediately after the German troops crossed the border, there would have been a tendency in Right-wing circles to work in favour of peace with Germany. His determined stand went a long way towards counteracting such a reaction, which was weakened in any case by the widespread belief that Germany would conquer Russia in a few weeks. The more successful the Soviet Government will be in resisting Germany, however, the more fears of spreading Communism over Europe are likely to grow in some quarters. For this reason, the German attack on Russia has increased the need for fighting appeasement.

Moreover, it seems probable at the time of writing that before long Hitler will embark upon a " peace offensive ". Possibly by the time these lines appear in print he will have broadcast a peace offer which on the surface may conceivably appear conciliatory. He could well afford to agree to the evacuation of the conquered countries, knowing very well that he would be in a position to reconquer them at any moment. It is essential that the public in Great Britain and in the United States should fully realise the utter folly of concluding peace with Hitler—or, for that matter, with any German Government—on any terms unless and until Germany's military power has been completely destroyed. The chances are that in the democratic countries the high degree of Government control adopted for the sake of national defence would be relaxed after the conclusion of peace, which would mean economic chaos and social troubles. A strong and undefeated Germany, with her disciplinarian system fully maintained, could easily take advantage of such a state of affairs for securing a swift victory over her opponents weakened by their internal difficulties.

Whether Hitler is victorious in Russia or not, his peace overtures must be rejected without hesitation. Only complete military victory over Germany could assure lasting peace. Every true supporter of freedom and peace must resist to the utmost the temptation of appeasement.

August 1941

THE END

Printed in Great Britain by R. & R. CLARK, LIMITED, *Edinburgh.*

71
72
74
75
76
77
79
83
88